MANAGING
PRESSURE
IN YOUR
MARRIAGE

FAMILYLIFE
HOMEBUILDERS
COUPLES SERIES

MANAGING PRESSURE IN YOUR MARRIAGE

DENNIS RAINEY AND ROBERT LEWIS

GROUP LEADER'S GUIDE

"UNLESS THE LORD BUILDS THE HOUSE
THEY LABOR IN VAIN WHO BUILD IT."
Psalm 127:1

Gospel Light

How to Let the Lord Build Your House and Not Labor in Vain

FamilyLife is a part of Campus Crusade for Christ International, an evangelical Christian organization founded in 1951 by Bill Bright. FamilyLife was started in 1976 to help fulfill the Great Commission by strengthening marriages and families and then equipping them to go to the world with the gospel of Jesus Christ. Our FamilyLife Marriage Conference is held in most cities throughout the United States and is one of the fastest-growing marriage conferences in America today. Information on all resources offered by FamilyLife may be obtained by either writing or calling us at the address and telephone number listed below.

The HomeBuilders Couples Series™: A small-group Bible study dedicated to making your family all that God intended.

Managing Pressure in Your Marriage—Group Leader's Guide
ISBN 0-8307-1631-9

Dennis Rainey, Executive Director
FamilyLife
P.O. Box 23840
Little Rock, AR 72221-3840
(501) 223-8663

A Ministry of Campus Crusade for Christ International
Bill Bright, Founder and President
Published by Gospel Light, Ventura, California 93006

Contents

Acknowledgments

Dave **B**oehi is a great warrior to be in a bunker with as we fight for the family. Dave, your editing skills, faithfulness and perseverance have resulted in another study that will impact thousands. You're a true difference-maker. Thanks for grabbing your weapon (computer) and hunkering down with us.

No study of excellence would be possible without field-testing and proofreading and Julie Denker has once again outdone herself in sharpening this resource. Thanks Julie, you're a winner!

No writer who also leads a church or ministry could do without a secretary who covers the essentials while he's away. To Mary Larmoyeux and Melissa Chance, thanks for juggling calls, deadlines, letters and a thousand demands with such gracious spirits.

To the Executive Team at FamilyLife, thanks. Thanks for slugging it out in the trenches of spiritual battle and giving 110 percent to the cause of Christ and the family. For organizing, raising money, managing people and money with integrity, selling these HomeBuilders studies, launching radio and hundreds of conferences, thanks to Merle and Lynn Engle, Don and Suzanne Dudgeon, Roger and Barbara Craft, Dave and Diana Daggett, Jerry and Sheryl Wunder, Blair and Debbye Wright and Ken and Nook Tuttle.

And, finally to our wives Sherard (Lewis) and Barbara (Rainey). Thanks for putting up with your man! For listening to us dream, ramble and overcommit ourselves. For being partners in ministering to families. And for being great wives and friends, you're the best!! (We realize there can't be two who are the best, but we argued about it and neither could put the other away!)

Introduction

About The HomeBuilders Couples Series™

What is the purpose of the HomeBuilders Series?

Do you remember the first time you fell in love? That junior high—or elementary school—"crush" stirred your affections with little or no effort on your part. We use the term "falling in love" to describe the phenomenon of suddenly discovering our emotions have been captured by someone delightful.

Unfortunately, our society tends to make us think that all loving relationships should be equally effortless. Thus, millions of couples, Christians included, approach their marriages certain that the emotions they feel will carry them through any difficulties. And millions of couples quickly learn that a good marriage does not happen automatically.

Otherwise intelligent people, who would not think of buying a car, investing money or even going to the grocery store without some initial planning, enter into marriage with no plan of how to make their marriage succeed.

But God has already provided the plan, a set of blueprints for a truly godly marriage. His plan is designed to enable two people to grow together in a mutually satisfying relationship and then to look beyond their own marriage to others. Ignoring this plan leads to isolation and separation between husband and wife—the pattern so evident in the majority of homes today. Even when great energy is expended, failure to follow God's blueprints results in wasted effort, bitter disappointment—and, in far too many cases, divorce.

In response to this need in marriages today, FamilyLife of Campus Crusade for Christ has created a series of small-group Bible studies for couples called The HomeBuilders Couples Series™. Although designed for use in small groups, the series is easily adaptable to larger groups such as adult Sunday School classes. It is planned to answer one question for couples:

How do you build a distinctively Christian marriage?

It is our hope that in answering this question with the biblical blueprints for building a home, we will see the development of growing, thriving marriages filled with the love of Jesus Christ.

FamilyLife of Campus Crusade for Christ is committed to strengthening your family. We hope The HomeBuilders Couples Series™ will assist you and your church as it equips couples to build godly homes.

What is this study intended to accomplish?

Couples who participate in these sessions will find that the experience:

• Stimulates them to examine what Scripture says about how to construct a solid, satisfying marriage.

• Allows them to interact with each other on a regular basis about significant issues in their marriages.

• Encourages them to interact with other couples, establishing mutual accountability for growth efforts.

• Motivates them to take specific actions which have been valuable to other couples desiring to build stronger homes.

• Creates accountability to others for growth in their marriages.

Why is accountability so important?

Accountability is a scriptural principle that tells us to "be subject to one another in the fear of Christ" (Ephesians 5:21). This means I choose to submit my life to the scrutiny of another person in order to gain spiritual strength, growth and balance.

Accountability means asking another person for advice. It means giving him or her the freedom to make honest observations and evaluations about you. It means you're teachable and approachable. True accountability involves letting another person into the interior of your life.

When people join a small group, they are opening themselves up for at least a small measure of accountability. Our experience has shown that many group members will make commitments to apply aspects of the studies to their lives, but will never follow through on those commitments. You, as a small-group leader, can help your group members get the most out of this study by establishing an environment of friendly accountability.

Look for some hints on establishing accountability in the "Tips for Leading Your Group" section.

What impact has The HomeBuilders Couples Series™ had on marriages?

Since we published the first HomeBuilders study in 1987 over 200,000 people have been challenged to build their homes on the Rock. We've continually heard stories about couples whose marriages were revitalized and in some cases were even saved. Here are some examples:

"We started our HomeBuilders group as a follow-up to the Video FamilyLife Marriage Conference presented at our church. We have developed a good openness among the group members. The study has brought problem areas to the surface and given us a greater sense of awareness of our responsibility toward our mates. One couple travels as far as an hour to attend!"

Pastor, Washington

"We're using *Building Your Marriage* and *Mastering Money in Your Marriage* in our Sunday School classes, both for newlyweds and as a marriage renewal class. I have seen couples open communication lines for the first time in a long time as a result of their involvement."

Bill Willits
Minister to Married Adults
First Baptist Church
Atlanta, Georgia

"We've led three studies now, and in each one of those we have seen ourselves grow. You really do co-learn."

Doug Grimm
Playa Del Rey, California

"I've built my family ministry around the FamilyLife Marriage Conference and the HomeBuilders. It makes biblically-minded, servant-minded people who are useful for advancing the kingdom and leadership of the kingdom."

Jeff Rhodes, Pastor
First Presbyterian Church
Winter Haven, Florida

"Nine weeks of the HomeBuilders class turned everything around in our relationship. It was a real miracle. The walls came down and the masks came off. We were able to discuss matters we had swept under the carpet years ago that our enemy was consistently using to destroy the love God had designed for us since the beginning of time....

"The HomeBuilders class really works. Here is why: HomeBuilders not only shows you why and tells you how; it teaches a way to alter your life-style so these great truths become a part of everyday living.

"We have truly overcome isolation and are building toward oneness in our marriage. We have learned how to yield to God and the leading of His Holy Spirit instead of our own selfish desires...the romance is back and the intimacy is growing every day. HomeBuilders has really given us the "wisdom" we were looking for in our marriage.

"It is absolutely the best thing that has ever happened to us since becoming Christians 18 years ago. It changed our lives at a time I was just ready to accept apathy for parts of my marriage, figuring there was no way to ever change."

Alan and Lanette Hauge
Playa Del Rey, California

How does this study fit into a strategy for building Christian marriages?

While this study has great value in itself, it is only the first step in a long-term process of growth. If people complete these sessions and then gradually return to their previous patterns of living, little or no good will result. Initiating and maintaining new directions in a marriage requires continued effort.

In addition, it is our belief that no couple can truly build a Christian home and marriage without a strong commitment and involvement in a local church. The church provides the daily spiritual direction and equipping necessary for a truly godly marriage.

FamilyLife is committed to changing the destiny of the family and providing quality resources to churches and individuals for building distinctively Christian marriages. In addition to The HomeBuilders Couples Series™, we offer:

• "FamilyLife Today," our daily radio show with Dennis Rainey. This half-hour broadcast offers biblical, practical tips for building your family with a foundation in Christ. Write us for local station air times and broadcast information.

• The FamilyLife Marriage Conference, a weekend getaway where couples can learn how to experience oneness in their marriages.

• The FamilyLife Parenting Conference, where parents learn practical strategies for raising their children to know and love the Lord.

• The Urban Family Conference, a shorter version of the FamilyLife Marriage Conference that is specially geared to the needs of African-American, Hispanic, and all ethnic families.

Can this study be used in other settings besides small groups?

Yes. With capable leadership, this study may be used effectively in other settings. For example:

• A counselor could use it with a couple.

• Two couples who know each other well could work through it together.

• You could go through the study with your mate. (We encourage you, however, to make your ultimate goal that of taking others through this study or participating in a small group. Accountability is essential for godly marriages.)

• A Sunday School leader can adapt it to a larger group setting. For some suggestions on how this can be done, refer to the section entitled, "Using This Study in a Sunday School Setting."

Does each session follow a format?

Yes. The following outline gives a quick look at how the sessions are structured:

Focus: a statement of the overall focus of the session you will be studying.

Warm Up: a time to help people get to know each other, review the past session, and begin the new study.

Blueprints: the biblical content of the session.

Construction: the application of the session—a small project done privately as a couple during the session.

HomeBuilders Principles: summary points made throughout the study.

Make a Date: a time for couples to decide when they will complete their **HomeBuilders Project**.

Recommended Reading: suggestions for use of

several books to get maximum value from the study.

HomeBuilders Project: a 60–90 minute project to be completed at home before the next session. Although this format may vary slightly from session to session, you should familiarize yourself with it so that you are aware of the purpose of each segment of the study. Explaining the segments to your group will also aid them in understanding the session's content.

How is the Bible used in this study?

As you proceed through this study, you'll notice that the Bible is regarded as the final authority on the issues of life and marriage. Although written centuries ago, this Book still speaks clearly and powerfully about the conflicts and struggles men and women face. The Bible is God's Word and contains His blueprints for building a godly home and for dealing with the practical issues of living.

While Scripture has only one primary interpretation, there may be several appropriate applications. Some of the passages used in this series were not originally written with marriage in mind, but they can be applied practically to the husband-wife relationship.

Encourage each group member to have a Bible along for each session. The *New American Standard Bible*, the *New International Version* and the *New King James Version* are three excellent English translations that make the Bible easy to understand.

What are the ground rules for these sessions?

These sessions are designed to be enjoyable and informative—and nonthreatening. Three simple ground rules will help ensure that everyone feels comfortable and gets the most out of the study:

1. Share nothing about your marriage which may embarrass your mate.

2. You may "pass" on any question you do not want to answer.

3. Complete the **HomeBuilders Projects** (questions for each couple to discuss and act on) between each session. Share one result at the next group meeting.

What is the purpose of this group leader's guide?

This book and the suggestions it contains are designed to start your creative juices flowing, not to cramp your style. You will undoubtedly come up with your own ways to instruct and teach this material. That's fine. Don't let these recommendations force you into a box.

If you find it difficult to be creative as a facilitator, however, this guide will relieve your fears. In it you will find ideas, questions and tips to help you keep the study moving. You will find that one good question on a hot topic can spawn great discussion and interaction.

The entire text of the personal study guide (including **Construction** and **HomeBuilders Projects**) is reprinted here, along with the tips for the leader and possible answers to the personal study guide questions. All answers, tips and notes appear in italics to distinguish them from the personal study guide material.

TIPS FOR LEADING A GROUP

What does it take to lead this study?

First, this is a couples' study in terms of leadership as well as group membership. You and your mate need to commit to each other and to God that this study will be a major priority for both of you.

Second, you and your mate will need to work together to enlist other couples to participate in the group.

Third, one of you will need to give time (at least one or two hours) each week to prepare for the session, while the other takes the initiative to stay in touch with group members and to handle all the details of hospitality.

And fourth, we recommend that you pray regularly for each couple in your group.

NOTE: Session Five in this study involves separating the husbands and wives into two separate groups. You will need to arrange for someone— your mate or another person—to lead the other group.

What is the leader's job?

Your role is that of "facilitator"—a directive guide who encourages people to think, to discover what Scripture says and to interact with others in the group. You are not a teacher or lecturer; your job is to help the group members glean biblical truth and apply it to their lives.

At the same time, however, you don't want to let group members ramble aimlessly or pool their ignorance. You'll need to familiarize yourself with the material so that you know where the discussion is headed and so you can provide answers when needed. The directions in this group leader's guide will help you keep each session moving.

What is the best setting for this group to meet?

Your living room is probably the best place to use for a small group. Inviting couples to your home is usually easier and friendlier than trying to get them to come to a room at church. You need a room where everyone can sit comfortably and see and hear each other.

Avoid letting couples or individuals sit outside the group; they will not feel included. The seating arrangement is very important to discussion and involvement. If your home will not work, see if another couple in the group is willing to host the sessions.

What about refreshments?

If you want a comfortable, relaxed setting that encourages people to get to know one another, something to sip and swallow is almost essential. But food should not become the focus of the session. Depending on the time of your meeting, you may find it works well to serve a beverage and light "munchies" as people arrive, then offer a dessert at the close of the study to encourage people to continue talking with each other for awhile.

What time schedule should we plan to follow?

A two-hour block is best. The actual study should take about 60–90 minutes, but allowing for the longer time period allows you to move at a more relaxed pace through each part of the session. During the school year, a session from 7:30–9:30 P.M. allows people to get home from work and get baby-sitters if needed.

Once the people in your group get to know each other and interaction gets underway, you may find it difficult to complete a session in the time allotted. It is not necessary that every question be covered, and many are intended to stimulate thought, not to result in exhaustive discussion and resolution of the issue. Be sensitive to your use of time, and be careful not to make comments about time pressure which will make the group feel rushed. For example:

When you need to move the discussion to the next item, say something like, "We could probably talk about that question the rest of the evening, but we need to consider several other important questions that bear on this issue."

When it's necessary to reduce or eliminate the time spent on a later question, simply say, "You can see that there are several more questions we could have moved on to discuss, but I felt we were making real progress, so I chose to spend some extra time on the earlier points."

You will find, as you prepare and review for each session, that some questions or sections are more relevant to your group than other portions of the study. Pace your study in such a way that those questions which must be addressed are not rushed.

You are the leader of your group and know the needs of the individual couples best. But keep in mind that the Holy Spirit will have an agenda for couples which you never know about.

"The mind of man plans his way, but the Lord directs his steps" (Proverbs 16:9). Do your best to prepare and pray over the session and then leave the results to God.

Be sure to protect the application (**Construction**) time of the session. Be aware of the common tendency to avoid taking action by getting embroiled in a discussion. Even if some issues are not fully resolved, encourage people to place the topic on hold and move on to planning specific actions to take. Personal application is the heart of this study.

Plan up to an additional 30 minutes for fellowship, 5 or 10 minutes before the study and the remainder after it. When you invite people, tell them to plan on the total time. This avoids having people rush off and not get acquainted.

Also, when you invite people to attend, let them know that the study will go for six sessions. People like to know for how long they are committing themselves.

How many couples should be in a study group?

Four to seven couples, including you and your mate, is the optimum group size. Fewer than four may put too much pressure on some individuals, stifling their freedom to grow. More than seven will reduce the quality of the relationships that can grow among all the couples involved, even though there may still be ample opportunity for couples to interact with each other and with other couples in the group.

Whom should we invite to participate?

The concepts in this study will benefit any couple, whether they are newlywed, engaged, married many years or even just looking ahead to the possibilities of marriage. Leading the group will be easier if your group is made up of couples at similar stages in their relationships. The more they have in common, the easier it will be for them to identify with one another and open up in sharing.

On the other hand, it can also be helpful for couples to gain a fresh viewpoint on marriage by interacting with other couples having significantly different experiences. In other words, if a couple is interested in building and maintaining a strong marriage, they belong in this study.

What if one partner doesn't want to participate?

Expect that some people, especially some husbands, will attend the first session wishing they were someplace else. Some will be there just because their mate or another couple nagged them to come. Some may be suspicious of a "Bible" study. Others may be fearful of revealing any weaknesses in their marriage. And some may feel either that their marriage is beyond help or that they do not need any help.

You can dispel a great deal of anxiety and resistance at the first session. Simply begin by mentioning that you know there are probably some who came reluctantly. Share a few reasons people may feel that way and affirm that, regardless of why anyone has come, you are pleased each person is there.

Briefly comment on how the concepts in this study have helped you and your marriage and express your confidence that each person will enjoy the study and benefit from it. Also, assure the group that at no time will anyone be forced to share publicly. What each person shares is his or her choice—no one will be embarrassed.

Can a non-Christian participate in this study?

The study is definitely targeted at Christians, but many non-Christian couples have participated in it. You may find a non-Christian couple or individual who wants to build a strong marriage and is willing to participate. Welcome the non-Christian into your group and seek to get to know the person during the early weeks of the study.

Sometime during the study, schedule a time to meet with this person or couple privately to explain the principles on which this study is built. Share Christ and offer an opportunity to receive Him as Savior and Lord. We recommend "The Four Spiritual Laws" to help you explain how a person can know God. This information is included as an appendix to the personal study guide and the group leader's guide.

Do you have any suggestions for guiding the discussion?

Keep the focus on what Scripture says, not on you or your ideas—or those of the group members, either. When someone disagrees with Scripture, affirm him or her for wrestling with the issue and point out that some biblical statements are hard to understand or to accept. Encourage the person to keep an open mind on the issue at least through the remainder of the study.

Avoid labeling an answer as "wrong"; doing so can kill the atmosphere for discussion. Encourage a person who gives a wrong or incomplete answer to look again at the question or the Scripture being explored. Offer a comment such as "That's really close" or "There's something else we need to see there." Or ask others in the group to respond.

How can I get all the people in my group to participate in the discussion?

• A good way to encourage a nonparticipator to respond is to ask him or her to share an opinion or a personal experience rather than posing a question that can be answered "yes" or "no" or that requires a specific correct answer.
• The overly talkative person can be kept in control by the use of devices that call for responses in a specific manner (and that also help group members get to know little things about each other):

"I'd like this question to be answered first by the husband of the couple with the next anniversary."

"...the wife of the couple who had the shortest engagement."

"...any husband who knows his mother-in-law's maiden name."

"...anyone who complained about doing the last session's project."

• Other devices for guiding responses from the group include:

Go around the group in sequence, asking each person to comment about a particular question without repeating what anyone else has said.

Ask couples to talk with each other about a question, then ask whichever partner has said the least so far in the session to report on his or her answer.

Limit answers to 1 or 2 sentences—or to 30 seconds each.

How can I establish an environment of accountability?

From the outset, emphasize the importance of completing the **HomeBuilders Project** after each session. These projects give couples the opportunity to discuss what they've learned and to apply it in their lives. The couples who complete these projects will get two or three times as much out of this study as will those who do not.

The most important thing you can do is to state at the end of the first session that at your next meeting you will ask each couple to share something they learned from the **HomeBuilders Project**. Then, at the next session, follow through on your promise. If the couples in your group know you are going to hold them accountable, they'll be more motivated to complete the projects. And they'll be glad they did!

Remember, though, to make this an environment of friendly accountability. You should emphasize how beneficial the projects are and how much the couples will grow in their marriage relationship if they complete them. State that you are not here to condemn, but to help. And when you begin the following session by asking each couple what they learned from the project, do it with an attitude of encouragement and forgiveness. Don't seek to embarrass anyone.

One way to establish friendly accountability and to help couples know each other better is to pair up the couples in your group and assign them to be prayer partners or accountability partners. Have them call each other at some point between group meetings to exchange prayer requests and to see if they've completed their projects.

Another possibility to consider is making a special effort to hold the men accountable to initiate work on the projects. You'd need to commit yourself to calling the men in between sessions.

What should I expect group members to do at the end of these sessions?

As you prepare this study, prayerfully consider each couple in your group and the most appropriate next step to recommend they take when the study is completed:

1. Encourage them to commit to participate in another HomeBuilders study, such as *Building Teamwork in Your Marriage* by Robert Lewis or *Building Your Mate's Self-Esteem*. (Dennis and Barbara Rainey have coauthored a best-selling book with this same title.) Decide whether you or someone else will lead the study and when you would schedule it. Since some people may not continue to the next study, it may be wise to schedule the other study after several more groups have completed this one. However, if you wait too long, you and your group members

may lose the momentum built through this study.

2. Some couples in your group may be candidates to lead their own group in studying *Managing Pressure in Your Marriage*. Raise this possibility, even though their first reaction may be "We don't know enough to be leaders!" Assure them that sharing what they have learned with others is the best way to continue learning. And, obviously, if *you* can lead this study, they certainly can as well. Remember, the more couples who go through this book, the more couples you will have ready for another one.

Expect many to continue on through The HomeBuilders Couples Series™. Relationships established during this study will cause most group members to want to continue.

3. For continued growth encourage your group to go through another HomeBuilders Couples Study. Other studies include *Building Your Marriage* by Dennis Rainey, *Building Your Mate's Self-Esteem* by Dennis and Barbara Rainey, *Building Teamwork in Your Marriage* by Robert Lewis, *Life Choices for a Lasting Marriage* by David Boehi, *Managing Money in Your Marriage* by Ron Blue, *Resolving Conflict in Your Marriage* by Bob and Jan Horner and *Growing Together in Christ* by David Sunde.

USING THIS STUDY IN A SUNDAY SCHOOL SETTING

Although this study is currently written for a small-group, home Bible study, with a few minutes of extra planning you can easily adapt it for a Sunday School class. Here are a few steps to take:

Step One: Commit yourself to the small-

group format. Many Sunday School classes are geared around a *teaching* format rather than a *small-group* format. In other words, class members learn biblical content from a speaker and have little interaction with each other. The success of this HomeBuilders study, however, depends upon the small-group dynamic, with class members learning the content by discussing Scriptures among themselves and by sharing personal experiences. As leader of the class, you'll need to be committed to making this small-group concept work.

Step Two: Explain to your class how this study is different from others. Tell them about the small-group format and about the purpose of the series. Challenge them to commit themselves to coming each week. And explain the need to set aside an hour between Sundays to complete the **HomeBuilders Projects**.

Another difference with a HomeBuilders study is the **Construction** project, in which each couple meets privately for a few minutes during the study. While the classroom may not provide visual privacy as couples talk, the sound of numerous couples talking at once makes it unlikely that anyone will overhear someone's private conversation. In some cases the results of the **Construction** work are to be shared. In a class situation, this sharing should be done in small groups—or ask for volunteers to share with the full class.

Step Three: Decide how you want to cover all the material in the allotted class time. These sessions are written to last for 60–90 minutes. Most Sunday School classes are an hour long—and that time normally includes announcements, singing and prayer. Here are three options to consider as you try to fit the

HomeBuilders study into the shorter time period:

1. *Eliminate—for just these few weeks—the normal singing and announcements.* If you follow the shorter time guideline for each segment of the sessions, all the content and projects can fit into a 60-minute session.

People who are used to slipping in late may need an extra nudge to get them there on time. The informal fellowship dimension, which is vital to helping people feel at home in the group, can be added to a degree before and after the session. However, the leader will need to be very sensitive to using that time wisely, since people will have other commitments that keep them from lingering.

2. *Look for ways to condense the actual study to about 45 minutes.* One way to accomplish this, of course, is to cut a few questions. Look through each session and determine what is most important to cover. Mark the questions you think could be eliminated. For example, perhaps you can choose just one question from a **Warm Up.**

If you have more than one small group in your class, another option is to divide questions (or verses) among different groups for discussion, then have them report briefly on their answers to the whole class.

3. *Divide each session in half and use two weeks of Sunday School for each one.* Go through each session ahead of time and determine a natural stopping place—at the end of one section of **Blueprints,** for example. You can pick up the session at that point the next week.

One thing to consider if you use this option is that you may need to come up with a new **Warm Up** question to use at the beginning of the second week for each session.

Step Four: Determine how you're going to *divide* the class. If you have fewer than nine couples, you could just have one group. But if your class is larger, we suggest dividing it. You could either assign each couple to one group that it will meet with during the entire study, or you could divide the class into different groups each week.

Step Five: Decide how you're going to *direct* the class. Do you want to appoint a leader for each group, or do you prefer guiding the discussion from up front? If you do want to guide the discussion, you could switch back and forth between having the individuals answer questions to the whole class and having them answer just within the small groups.

Step Six: Arrange your physical setting. Use a room where interaction in small groups and couples can easily occur. Leave adequate open space where people can mingle casually before and after the session. Set up chairs around tables or just in circles of six to eight. For variety in some sessions, you may want to set the chairs in a large semicircle (with more than one row if necessary). Avoid straight rows that leave people seeing only the backs of heads.

Plan to use a chalkboard, overhead projector or flip chart occasionally to emphasize key points, to focus attention on key questions or Scriptures and/or to write instructions for assignments to be done by individuals, couples or small groups. Be cautious about overusing these tools; they can set a "classroom" tone that may inhibit some people from full participation.

Special Note About Session Five in This Study: In this session you'll divide the husbands and wives into separate groups. If a second room is not available in the church building during the Sunday School hour, we suggest you arrange for either the husbands' or the wives' group to meet in a nearby home or restaurant.

Step Seven: Decide how you'll set up an atmosphere of accountability. While the **HomeBuilders Projects** are done by couples at home, it is vital that a larger group size does not allow people to escape accountability for completing the assignments. One option is to pair each couple with another couple with whom they agree to be accountable. Another plan is to divide the class into two or more teams. Each week, require couples to turn in an affidavit that they completed their project. Tabulate the results. The team with the lowest completion rate must provide some agreed-upon benefit (preferably edible) for the winning team at the end of the series.

Step Eight: Make plans for your group to attend the FamilyLife Marriage Conference in your area. It's a whole lot of fun for your group to get away together at one of our FamilyLife Marriage Conference locations. Call 1-800-333-1433 for information on group discounts and free brochures.

ABOUT THIS GROUP LEADER'S GUIDE

Be sure to read all the group leader's guide comments for each session before you lead it.

Each question that group members will answer is positioned in the **left-hand margin**. Its **corresponding answer** is printed in italics in the main body of the page **below the answer space**.

The entire text of the personal study guide is included in this book. This text is printed in normal type, while comments, answers to questions and tips **for the leader are printed in italics**. This italicized leader's material does not appear in the personal study guide.

---

b. What do you think you learned about prayer when you were a child? What attitudes and habits did you pick up?

▶**b.**
_____
_____
_____
_____

POSSIBLE ANSWER: Some people may realize that their prayers today are very similar to the ones they prayed as a child. Others may have grown up in homes where nobody prayed, and so they learned that prayer is not important.

Blueprints

(20 minutes)

*The following **Blueprints** section is designed to highlight some common barriers to prayer and some major benefits, then to outline some of the major components of prayer.*

I. THE BARRIERS TO PRAYER

*TIP: Since the **Warm Up** may have already touched on some of the negative things people in the group learned about prayer, you may not want to spend too much time here. It's important to touch*

The most important information for you is the **answers**, **tips**, **comments** and **notes**. To make it easy for you to focus on this information, it has been placed prominently in the main body of the page.

on the barriers to prayer, so that your group members can identify what keeps them from praying more.

A. What do you think the average Christian thinks about prayer? What keeps people from praying more than they do?

▶**A.**

POSSIBLE ANSWER: *Christians often have bad attitudes about prayer, and these attitudes keep them from praying more. They think prayer is boring, difficult, repetitive, ineffective. Some Christians wonder if prayer is really necessary; if God knows everything, why do we need to pray? Or they may wonder why God doesn't seem to answer their prayers more often. Another reason Christians may not pray is that they don't know how to do it.*

You have been provided **an answer and an answer space**. You may use that space to write your answer to the question and **any additional notes** that will help you adapt or direct that question to the individuals in the group.

B. Why do you think Christian couples often fail to spend much time together in prayer?

▶**B.**

POSSIBLE ANSWER: *Christian couples often know they should pray together, but they just don't do it. They don't make prayer together a regular habit, and they let other activities and priorities take precedence. Another reason they may not pray is that they don't feel comfortable doing it.*

HomeBuilders Principles

HomeBuilders Principle #1: Good decisions can make pressure reasonable and bearable.

HomeBuilders Principle #2: Our decisions are a mirror of our values; they should reflect our desire to put God first in our lives.

HomeBuilders Principle #3: Wise decisions are born out of wise counsel—from God (the Scriptures) and from godly advisers—and from prayer together as a couple.

HomeBuilders Principle #4: Life does not consist of possessions, but of relationships—with God, with our families and with our fellow human beings.

HomeBuilders Principle #5: Couples need to be honest with each other about the influence of materialism in their lives.

HomeBuilders Principle #6: Couples need to seek contentment within the means which God has provided.

HomeBuilders Principle #7: Nothing is as wearisome as wandering through life.

HomeBuilders Principle #8: Unacknowledged sin has a price: Exhaustion! Real rest is found in a clear conscience.

HomeBuilders Principle #9: In some areas of life, letting go may be the best strategy. Couples can decrease pressure in their lives by deciding to cut down on their responsibilities, expectations and commitments.

HomeBuilders Principle #10: Advance preparation is the best pressure-release valve for a new marital season.

HomeBuilders Principle #11: Couples need to make their sexual relationship a high priority.

HomeBuilders Principle #12: To build true sexual intimacy, defeat selfishness by focusing on what your mate needs.

HomeBuilders Principle #13: Freedom in marriage is found by embracing what is right, not in redefining what is right.

HomeBuilders Principle #14: If your Christianity is not defined practically, it will be practically worthless.

HomeBuilders Principle #15: A couple cannot face the pressures of today's amoral culture unless they walk together in agreement with their standards.

A Word About Pressure

All **of us** face pressure. Some of it is just the natural "stuff" of everyday life. But some of it isn't. It's brought upon us by our own lack of planning, poor choices, wrong values, unresolved conflicts and leaving God out of our lives.

We want to help you reduce pressure by addressing problems we all face in some fresh new ways using the timeless truths of Scripture. *Managing Pressure in Your Marriage* will help you as a couple come to grips with how you make decisions, how you agree on moral boundaries, and how to face "new seasons" and thus new issues and problems in your marriage. This study won't provide you with all the answers but it will aid you in the process of hammering out your own convictions and solutions as you navigate through life's circumstances.

As topics go, *Managing Pressure in Your Marriage* could touch a lot of subjects; far more than we could address in this short six-session study. We've chosen to go after some issues that few are addressing and fewer still are pointing people back to the Scriptures to solve.

Enjoy these sessions. Do the projects. Talk. Interact. Hammer out what you believe based upon God's Word. But regardless, get involved with your spouse in the process of addressing six of life's most pressing issues. We know the end result will be worth it!

Robert Lewis and
Dennis Rainey

DECISION MAKING AND PRESSURE

OBJECTIVES

In this session you will help your group members:

- Discuss some of the typical pressures they face daily;
- Understand the critical link between pressure and the decisions we make; and
- Learn some key principles of good decision making.

OVERALL COMMENTS

1. If you haven't read through "A Word About Pressure" in the Introduction, be sure to do so. The first paragraph from that page sums up the theme of this study: "All of us face pressure. Some of it is just the natural 'stuff' of everyday life. But some of it isn't. It's brought upon us by our own lack of planning, poor choices, wrong values, unresolved conflicts and leaving God out of our lives."

   This session establishes this theme by leading the group members to talk about the pressure they face and about the ways their decisions affect this pressure. This may be a new concept for some people who haven't thought through the way they make decisions, and the consequences those decisions can have.

2. Subsequent sessions will focus on specific areas in which we need to make solid, biblical decisions. Your group members should understand that this study is not a comprehensive treatment on pressure, but it should give them a biblical framework to use as they think through "pressure points" in their lives.

STARTING THE FIRST SESSION

1. Start the session on time, even if everyone is not yet present. Briefly share a few positive feelings about leading this study.

    • Express your interest in strengthening your own marriage and dealing positively with managing pressure.

    • Admit that your marriage and the way you manage pressure in your marriage are not perfect.

    • State that the concepts in this study have been helpful in your marriage.

    • Recognize that various individuals or couples may have been reluctant to come (pressured by spouse or friend, wary of a "Christian" group, sensitive about problems with marriage and/or conflict, stressed by a schedule that makes it difficult to set aside time for this series, etc.).

    • Thank group members for their interest and willingness to participate.

2. Hand out the personal study guides if you have not already done so, and give a quick overview of The HomeBuilders Couples Series™ and the guides. Briskly leaf through the guide and point out three or four topics and the benefits of studying them. Don't be

afraid to do a little selling here—people need to know how they personally are going to profit from the study. They also need to know where this series will take them, especially if they are even a little bit apprehensive about the group.

Making wise decisions is essential in resolving the pressures we face in life.

(15-20 minutes)

This first **Warm Up** *exercise is important—you want your group members to start talking with each other and also to get to know each other better. Accordingly, the amount of time suggested for this* **Warm Up** *is greater than for those in the following sessions.*

Choose one of the following options for your group. If your group members do not know each other well, Option A would work well as a "get to know you" time. If they are already familiar with each other, Option B might be a better choice.

Option A

1. Take a few minutes to get to know one another. Interview another couple in your group for five minutes and then introduce them to the rest of the group.

▶ **1.**

a. Name, where they live, years married, children, and vocation.

▶ **a.**

b. Something funny or unique that happened at their wedding or on their honeymoon.

c. What they hope to get out of this study.

b.

c.

Use this space to take notes about the other couple:

Option *B*

1. Think back over the past 12 months. What have been 1-3 highlights of your year, and why?

1.

2. Share with the group the low point of your year, and tell how it created pressure in your life.

2.

3. Share what you hope to get out of the study.

3.

I. Living in a
Pressure-Cooker World

(10-15 minutes)

COMMENTS: *The questions in this section have no right or wrong answers. They are designed to open up discussion in your group and also to set a tone for the entire six-session study.*

A. What circumstances or expectations cause you to feel pressure during a typical week—at work or at home?

▶ **A.**

TIP: *To get discussion started, share some answers yourself, then ask other group members to contribute.*

B. How do you typically react to pressure? How does it affect you physically and emotionally? How does it affect your personality?

▶ **B.**

TIP: *Encourage members to be honest here. Be authentic yourself, and share a situation from your own life.*

C. What do you typically do to reduce pressure in your life?

▶ C.

TIP: *You may ask them if they do anything to reduce pressure—a lot of us just go through life "under the pile." Ask them to share their most effective tips for pressure reduction!*

II. How Decisions Affect the Pressure We Experience

(15-20 minutes)

CASE STUDY

Jim and Lisa enjoyed their life in the Midwestern town where they had both grown up. Jim managed the local office of a national insurance firm and did it well. He didn't earn a large salary, but housing in their town was pretty cheap, so his earnings were enough to allow Lisa to stay home with their two young children. They belonged to a church they both enjoyed, and their parents lived within 10 minutes of their neighborhood.

Then Jim received a visit from his district manager. "I'm moving up to the head office in New York," the manager said. "I need to find a replacement, and you're my first choice."

For Jim, this seemed like the opportunity of a lifetime. The new position would mean a substantial increase in salary and would even give him the opportunity to do some traveling. The only drawback was that the family would have to move to St. Louis, about three hours away.

Jim knew he would miss his family and friends, but he was excited about the prospect of advancing his career.

By the time Jim arrived home that night, he had practically decided to take the new job. "This is my chance to move up the ladder," he told Lisa. "I even mentioned the possibility to a couple of my business clients, and they said I might not get an opportunity like this again."

"But I don't want to leave," Lisa protested. "I'm happy here—I don't want to leave my family and friends."

"But we'll never have the chance to get ahead if we stay here. This way we can afford to get a larger house. We'll be able to sell our old car and get a minivan and with the kids getting bigger, you know we need one."

Eventually Jim won her over. Three months later they found themselves in a new home, a new city and a new minivan. But now they were facing a new set of problems they hadn't anticipated.

First, there was the job, which turned out to require quite a bit more than "a little traveling." Jim was often out of town three or four days a week, and often he needed to work on Saturdays as well. Lisa sometimes felt like a single mother, and it seemed worse because she was unable to lean on her family to help with the kids as she had before. On top of that, she became pregnant again.

They missed their families and their friends terribly. They joined a good church, but their lives were so hectic now that they had a hard time meeting new friends there. Jim was often so tired on Sundays that he just wanted to sleep in anyway. And he was out of town so often on weekday nights that they decided they couldn't commit to joining a couples' Bible study.

Their new life went on like this for a year, and then came the big bombshell: Jim's company was sold to a larger conglomerate which already had a district manager in that area. Jim's work was highly regarded by his new employers, however, and once again he was offered a new position as a regional manager working out of Chicago. "We need people like you, Jim," he was told. "In a few years you'll probably be moving on up to the New York office."

A. What pressures were Jim and Lisa feeling as they made their first decision about moving?

▶**A.** _____

_____

_____

_____

ANSWER: *Jim was feeling "career pressure." He felt he needed to be moving up the corporate ladder, that he'd be a failure if he wasn't advancing. He even thought he might be passed over in the future if he didn't take this opportunity now. In addition, both Jim and Lisa were feeling financial pressure— they had enough for their basic needs, but not much more.*

B. In what ways did Jim and Lisa's decision increase the pressures they felt?

▶**B.** _____

_____

_____

ANSWER: *They didn't fully realize how their decision would change their life-style. They didn't have a realistic idea of what Jim's job would involve and how it would affect them. They actually ended up with more pressure in their lives than they had before.*

Much of the pressure we feel each day is unavoidable—it's a part of life. But the decisions we make in response to the situations that cause pressure are critical. We can make decisions that reduce pressure and help us cope with it. Or we can make decisions that make the pressure worse than what we're presently feeling.

HOMEBUILDERS PRINCIPLE

Good decisions can make pressure reasonable and bearable.

1

C. How does our culture give people the idea that "climbing the corporate ladder" is so important?

C.

ANSWER: *In our culture we are subtly told that success is measured by our position, our influence, our possessions. It's easy to compare ourselves to other people—whether those people are friends, coworkers or even imaginary characters in the media—and find ourselves lacking.*

D. In the end, many of the decisions we make are influenced by our personal values—what we consider important. What factors should Jim and Lisa consider as they make their decision about whether to move to Chicago?

▶**D.**

ANSWERS: *They should consider whether career growth is worth the price they may have to pay in their marriage and family life. They should consider the importance of being part of a good church that encourages them to grow spiritually. They probably need a greater commitment to spiritual growth. They also need to decide how important relationships with family and friends are to them and to consider that factor in their decision.*

Construction

(to be completed as a couple)
(10 minutes)
*This **Construction** project helps a couple see the link of how they make decisions and how their parents made decisions while growing up. They will also discover that each spouse may make decisions differently.*

A. How did you observe your parents making decisions as you grew up? Share any good or bad lessons you learned from them.

▶**A.**

When two individuals enter into marriage, they often discover that they have different decision-making styles than their mates. One person may make decisions quickly, while the other deliberates for a few days. One may take a factual approach to the decision; the other makes it more emotionally. The result can be conflict and pressure.

B. In what ways do you and your mate differ when it comes to how you make decisions?

▶ **B.**

III. PRINCIPLES OF GOOD DECISION MAKING

(15-25 minutes)

TIP: *If you have time, have group members share one thing they talked about with their mates during the **Construction** project.*

In our lives each of us will make thousands of decisions. They set our direction, reveal our values and determine our course. Decisions determine our destiny and play a key role in how we handle the pressures we face each day. Yet few people ever receive formal training in how to make good decisions. Even fewer ever take the time to hammer out a biblically based strategy for decision making—one that is based on how God wants us to make our choices.

A. Principle #1: Put God first.

Read Matthew 6:33,34. How would you apply this truth to decision making?

▶

ANSWER: *We need to seek God and His wisdom whenever we make our decisions. This is the first, and most important, step. One person shared that, when facing a difficult decision he would ask, "What would Jesus do in this situation?" The Scriptures exhort us to lead lives that are pleasing to God in all ways.*

HOMEBUILDERS PRINCIPLE

Our decisions are a mirror of our values; they should reflect our desire to put God first in our lives.

2

B. Principle #2: Obey the Scriptures.

1. Upon what does Matthew 7:24-27 say we are to base our decisions? How can this affect the pressures you face in your marriage and family life?

1.

ANSWER: *We are to make decisions based upon God's Word. If you obey God's Word, then you will be able to withstand the pressures you will inevitably face in life If you fail to obey God's Word, then you will not be able to withstand the pressures.*

TIP: *Ask if anyone is willing to share a wrong decision they made that caused more pressure.*

2. In many areas, Scripture is so clear that deciding what to do should not take you long. For example, the Bible states in Exodus 20:14 and many other passages that adultery is a sin; God is crystal clear on that issue. What are some other examples of decisions that should be easy to make because of Scripture's clear guidance?

2.

ANSWERS: *Lying, stealing, cheating, loving things, etc.*

TIP: *Ask them to comment on how the Ten Commandments help us make good decisions. What are the benefits of obeying them?*

C. Principle #3: Seek God's wisdom—together. For some decisions, you may not be able to find a verse or passage from Scripture that provides clear guidance. When this happens, you will need to seek the Lord together as a couple and ask for wisdom. Here are some suggestions for how to go about seeking the Lord as a couple:

1. Pray for guidance. Read Proverbs 3:5-7.

a. How does this passage apply to making decisions?

a.

ANSWER: *When we trust completely in God and look to Him for guidance, He is able to give us understanding and wisdom that we could not have otherwise.*

b. Why do many couples find it difficult to pray *together* about decisions they face?

b.

ANSWERS: *Some couples have not together developed a good spiritual life. Some people may be prideful and don't want to admit their need for God or their inability to handle the situation on their own. Or they may not know how to pray together. Also, they may not ever spend much time together in prayer, and therefore it's awkward to pray together when making a difficult decision.*

c. How could you as a couple better prepare for decisions through prayer?

▶ **c.** _____

_____

_____

ANSWER: Commit to each other that you will seek the Lord together as an early step when making a decision. While praying, listen to the voice of the Holy Spirit in your hearts. Is God leading you in a certain direction?

TIP: You might want to demonstrate to your group how you pray about a decision or problem.

▶ **2.** _____

_____

_____

2. Honestly evaluate your options. Read Luke 14:27-32. Why do you think so many people fail to "calculate the cost" as they contemplate a decision?

ANSWERS: Many people are so driven by their desire to pursue a certain course that they just don't care what the consequences are, or they think that they will be able to easily handle any problem. Also, they may not take the time needed to think through the probable consequences of certain decisions or actions, or they fail to admit honestly how they'll react to different pressures.

3. Seek wise counsel.

▶ **a.** _____

_____

_____

a. Read Proverbs 12:15; 13:20; 15:22. What typically prevents people from following the advice in these verses?

ANSWERS: They're prideful (they want their way, not God's way) and don't want to seek the counsel of others; they don't know any "wise men" they can get help from.

b. How can you determine whom to approach for counsel?

▶ **b.**

ANSWER: *You can spot wise people and fools from the track records they leave. Look for a counselor who leans on prayer and has a history of walking with God in obedience to Scripture. Also, look for someone who has been through a situation similar to the one you face.*

4. Decide which of your choices is the wisest and commit your decision together to the Lord. Read Ecclesiastes 4:9-12. Why are you better off making your decisions together as a couple?

▶ **4.**

ANSWER: *Since decisions in a marriage involve both partners, both partners should be involved in making the decisions. That way, you'll get both points of view as you make your decision. God often puts together a man and a woman with different temperaments and decision-making approaches, and they make better decisions together than they would separately. Also, you often can act as safeguards to one another to avoid bad decisions. If one spouse wants to pursue a certain course and the other feels strongly that it's a bad decision, the couple probably should put off the decision and look at it more closely.*

TIP: *Ask anyone to share how they've found this true in their marriage—be specific.*

$\mathcal{H}$OMEBUILDERS $\mathcal{P}$RINCIPLE

Wise decisions are born out of
wise counsel—from God (the
Scriptures) and from godly
advisers—and from prayer
together as a couple.

3

IV. CONCLUSION

(5 minutes)

To manage pressure in marriage, it's essential that a couple understands and practices good decision making. You can use the principles learned in this session for a multitude of decisions in your life.

In the remaining sessions you will study five crucial areas that bring enormous pressure to families today. If they are not handled properly, they can crush a marriage relationship.

COMMENTS: *Ask each couple to look at the* **Make a Date** *section of the personal study guide, and to agree on a time this week to complete* **HomeBuilders Project #1** *together. Encourage them to set aside 45 minutes to an hour to respond to the items individually and discuss their answers together.*

Each **HomeBuilders Project** *is absolutely essential for couples to do together during the week. Emphasize that this is not homework to earn a passing grade, but a highly significant time of interaction that will improve communication and understanding as the couple builds their marriage according to God's blueprints.*

Point out that the questions start out fairly non-threatening, but quickly focus on potentially sensitive issues. The intention is not to start arguments, but to stimulate honest reflection and interaction. While not every question will affect every couple in the same way, the time spent thinking and talking will be more than worthwhile for any couple.

Remind the group that at the next session you will ask each couple to share one thing they discovered or discussed during the **HomeBuilders Project.** *Also, remind group members to bring their calendars to the next session as an aid in scheduling their next date with their mates.*

OPTION: *You may want to pair each couple with another couple with whom they will agree to be accountable to complete the* **HomeBuilders**

Projects. *Have the couples tell each other when they will be doing the projects. The couples can then call each other later to see how the projects went, or you can have them meet with each other for a few minutes at the start of the next session.*

Set a date with your mate to meet in the next few days to complete **HomeBuilders Project #1.** Your leader will ask at the next session for you to share one thing from this experience.

Date	Time	Location

Recommended Reading

COMMENTS: *Call attention to the **Recommended Reading** section. The book or books listed at the end of each session are not required, but are recommended to reinforce and expand the concepts dealt with in the group session. Encourage couples to locate these resources and read them before the next session. One effective idea is for one spouse to read aloud to the other, either in the morning before going to work or in the evening before going to sleep.*

Staying Close, by Dennis Rainey.

Countless married Americans end up living alone—in the same house! Years of conducting FamilyLife Conferences have convinced Dennis Rainey, executive director of FamilyLife, that isolation is the number-one problem in marriages today. This book provides a positive, workable strategy for keeping your marriage vital and intimate.

Life Choices for a Lasting Marriage, by David Boehi.

One of the studies in The HomeBuilders Couples Series™, this small-group course will challenge you to make "Life Choices"—key commitments—that will build the foundation of a lasting marriage.

Lead the group in a closing prayer. If you know the group members well enough, you may feel comfortable having them spend a few minutes praying for one another's ability to withstand marital pressures in the coming week.

Provide light refreshments and invite couples to linger and chat with each other. Informal opportunities to build relationships are a key ingredient in the success of this series. If necessary, shorten the study time in this session so that people do not feel exhausted or pressed to leave quickly.

HomeBuilders Project #1

1. Review Session One and write down the most important concept or truth you learned.

2. Take a look at the principles for decision making outlined in Section III of **Blueprints**. What do you think are your greatest strengths and weaknesses in this area of your life?

Strengths:

Weaknesses:

3. What action do you need to take in order to improve your decision-making ability? (For example: keep a daily prayer time, involve your spouse more in decisions, etc.)

4. What do you think are your mate's greatest strengths and weaknesses in decision making?

Strengths:

Weaknesses:

5. What two or three pressures are you currently facing that a wise decision might alleviate?

6. Are there any decisions you've made lately which you need to reevaluate—choices which have caused additional pressure on you, your mate, or your family? If so, list them here.

7. What is one thing you'd like to implement in your marriage as a result of this study?

INTERACT AS A COUPLE: 30 MINUTES

1. Share your answers from the individual portion of this project.

2. As you look at the subject of decision making, discuss:

What is one thing you're *doing right* as a couple?

What is one thing you need to *stop* doing?

What is one thing you need to *start* doing?

3. Take a look at your weekly schedule. What are some decisions you could make that would alleviate any time pressure you feel?

4. Close in prayer together. Pray for one another, for wisdom, and for any decisions you need to make.

Remember to bring your calendar to the next session so you can **Make a Date.**

THE PRESSURE OF MATERIALISM

OBJECTIVES

In this session you will lead your group members as they:

- Discuss the impact of materialism on a couple's financial decisions and their families;
- Take an honest look at their own materialistic attitudes;
- Examine what the Bible says about materialism; and
- Determine some key decisions they can make to reduce the pressure of materialism in their finances.

OVERALL COMMENTS

1. Materialism is so pervasive and so deeply rooted in our culture today that many of us are blind to the extent that it has infected us. One of your primary tasks as leader in this session will be gently but steadily to force your group members to examine themselves. They may not like what they see, and they may even deny it, but the discussion should challenge them to evaluate a substantial source of pressure in their lives: materialism.

2. Some of your group members may be a bit defensive as they discuss materialism. For example, during the case study, which focuses on a decision to purchase a new home, someone who has recently bought a new home may speak up and give reasons why this was a good decision. In other words, they may be justifying to the group a purchase they've recently made. If this occurs, tell the group that the main purpose of the session is just to ask ourselves some difficult questions that force us to think through our values and priorities. What one couple decides is best for them may not be what another couple would decide. The key is whether a couple is submissive to the Lord and honest with themselves about the influence of materialism in their decision.

3. As you work through this session, as well as the others that follow, remember the overall theme of the study: how our decisions can increase the pressure we feel in our marriage.

Focus

Couples can reduce pressure in their marriages by taking a hard look at how materialism influences their financial decisions.

Warm-Up

(10-20 minutes)

1. Choose one of the following:

a. Tell about something dumb you've seen or heard other people do with money.

a.

b. Share something dumb you've done with your money.

b.

c. Share a childhood scheme that you had for making money. What was the result?

▶ **c.**

2. Why do you think so many couples report that finances are a major source of pressure in their marriages?

▶ **2.**

3. How have you experienced pressure as a couple as you have managed your financial resources? If you are willing, tell about your first conflict over money, or a recent difficult discussion you've had.

▶ **3.**

1. WHAT IS MATERIALISM?

(10-15 minutes)

A close look at our country's financial status will reveal that an astonishing number of Americans are in debt. Unfortunately, this places a great deal of pressure on today's marriages.

There are many things a couple can do to improve their financial management skills. Many couples, for example, do not keep even a simple budget to keep track of their spending. What's really needed, however, is for us to take a hard look at the materialistic attitudes that pressure us into poor financial decisions.

The second college edition of *Webster's New World Dictionary* provides some interesting definitions of the word "materialism":

> ...the doctrine that comfort, pleasure, and wealth are the only or highest goals or values...the tendency to be more concerned with material than with spiritual or intellectual goals or values.

A. How can you tell if a person is materialistic?

▶**A.** _____

_____

_____

ANSWER: *If his or her energies are used up in pursuit of comfort and possessions. If he or she is overly concerned with appearance and comparison.*

B. Can someone be poor and also materialistic?

▶**B.** _____

_____

_____

ANSWER: *Yes! People with little money can be just as preoccupied with what they have or don't have—and therefore materialistic—as people with a lot of money can be.*

C. State whether you agree or disagree with the following statement and why: "Christians are nearly as materialistic as anyone else."

▶ **C.**

ANSWER: *This is mostly a subjective question, but our opinion is that many Christians are nearly as materialistic as other people. Many people think they are not materialistic, but if they took an honest look at their life-style and their preoccupations, they might think otherwise. In addition, even though we complain about the state of our economy and about our economic problems, our society is still one of the wealthiest on the earth. We live in a culture that is based so much on consumption and spending that we are materialistic in ways we would hardly recognize unless we visited a Third World country.*

TIP: *Whatever an individual says, be sure he or she explains the reason for the answer. Get them to back up their opinions. To help the discussion along, you might want to force some debate by purposely disagreeing with what group members say. For example, if someone agrees with the statement, say, "But I thought the Bible says we're not supposed to have a love for money."*

II. The Causes and Results of Materialism

(20-30 minutes)

A. Why is it so easy to be materialistic in our culture today?

▶ **A.**

ANSWER: *We live in a culture of consumption. We are constantly bombarded by media messages urging us to purchase things. Advertisements seduce us every day with messages designed to make us think we will feel better if we just buy a new car, a new perfume, or even a certain brand of soft drink. Television programs show us the "Lifestyles of the Rich and Famous." It's nearly impossible to escape our culture's preoccupation with materialism.*

TIP: *If you want, bring out some magazines and have the group members look for the messages encouraging them to buy things. Or show some recent television commercials on your VCR and talk about the messages we absorb as we watch television.*

B. If you can, tell about one purchase you made during the last 6-12 months. Share about a time when you made a poor decision about a purchase, investment or finances because of the cultural pressure of materialism.

▶ **B.**

TIP: *Be prepared to share an experience of your own to start off the discussion if necessary. Briefly discuss how we can so shrewdly justify our actions to ourselves.*

C. Read the following case study:

CASE STUDY

Like many young couples, Robert and Maria began their married life in an apartment. During their first four years of marriage, they both worked, and eventually they managed to save enough money for a small down payment on their own home. Soon after Maria gave birth to their first child, they purchased a three-bedroom home in a neighborhood where quite a few other young couples lived. The house wasn't especially large, but it seemed adequate to meet their needs. They also wanted to be able to live on one income, and they were able to do that with this house.

During the next several years, Robert and Maria had two more children, and they enjoyed refurbishing the home. Robert continued to take on more responsibility at work, and his income increased accordingly. When their youngest child entered kindergarten, Maria decided to take a part-time job as a preschool teacher.

After they had been in the home for nine years, Robert and Maria began to feel a bit restless. "This house is starting to feel small," Maria said. "The kids could use more room to play and entertain their friends."

It seemed as if all the couples they knew were moving into their second homes. "You should see the house that the Spragues moved into," Robert said. "Just walking through it made me jealous!"

Robert and Maria spent a few weekends with a realtor and came upon the house of their dreams. It had just been built, and it offered four bedrooms, 3,000 square feet, a sun room, a huge backyard, crown molding throughout the house, and brand-new appliances in the kitchen. The problem was the price. Their house payment would more than double, and the only way they could afford that would be for Maria to find a new job with more hours.

Their budget would be pretty tight, but they were convinced that house would be worth any sacrifice. "This is the home I've always wanted," Maria said. "I just know we'll be happy here."

1. What were some of the attitudes and pressures that led Robert and Maria to decide to purchase the second home?

▶ **1.**

ANSWER: *They felt pressure from having a small house, and that pressure was magnified because they probably had too much furniture in it. They also felt pressure because their friends were moving into larger homes. They felt a restlessness after being in one house for nine years. And in the back of their minds was the "dream home" they believed would make them happy.*

2. What kinds of pressures are they likely to experience as a result of this decision?

▶ **2.**

ANSWER: *They will go from a situation where they could afford what they needed to one where they are barely keeping their heads above water. Once in the home, they'll probably feel pressure to purchase other things, like furniture, or yard work, to "keep up" with their neighbors. And with Maria spending more time at work, she'll feel pressure in her relationship with her children.*

3. How did Robert and Maria's decision reflect their values?

▶ **3.**

ANSWER: *The decision reveals a possible preoccupation with maintaining a certain life-style. While some of their reasons for purchasing the second home may have been good, they were too worried about how they compared with their friends. As a result, they were willing to risk paying a high price for it in terms of their family relationships and their financial security.*

TIP: *Ask, "Would Robert and Maria have said they valued their kids more than material comfort?" "Do you think that their decision actually proved they valued other things more important?" Be careful with these questions, but encourage couples to think about the difference between stated values and their real values.*

D. In what ways has the tendency to compare yourself with others affected you and your financial decisions?

▶ **D.**

TIP: *A more specific follow-up question could be: "Can you think of a time that you really wanted to buy something that someone else had?" Or, "What is something you wanted recently and you felt you just had to have?"*

E. What do the following Scriptures say about materialism and handling money?

► E.

1. 1 Timothy 6:6-10

► 1.

ANSWER: *This passage is full of wisdom about finances and materialism. It tells us that we should be content with having our basic needs met. By pointing to the fact that we brought nothing into the world and we will take nothing out of it, it reminds us that we should have an eternal mind-set and make pleasing God our priority. It also warns us to avoid a love for money and a desire for riches. Materialism is a snare. We experience foolish and harmful desires that plunge us into ruin and destruction, and we wander away from the faith.*

NOTE: *Don't look at 1 Timothy 6:11,12 at this point; you'll examine those verses later in this session.*

2. Luke 12:15-21

► 2.

ANSWER: *These verses tell us that our life does not consist of possessions but in being rich toward God. It points us to what is truly important.*

3. Matthew 13:18-23 (with particular emphasis on verse 22)

▶ **3.**

ANSWER: *God wants His Word to bear fruit in our lives. But it's easy to allow "the worry of the world, and the deceitfulness of riches" to choke the growth in our lives and render us fruitless.*

HOMEBUILDERS PRINCIPLE

Life does not consist of possessions, but of relationships—with God, with our families and with our fellow human beings.

4

Construction

(to be completed as a couple)
(5-10 minutes)
Complete the following exercise individually and then share your answers with your mate:

Materialism: A Self-appraisal

	Strongly Disagree	Disagree	Undecided	Agree	Strongly Agree
1. I would be happier if I could double my income.	1	2	3	4	5
2. I really love buying things.	1	2	3	4	5
3. I find myself often thinking about new things I'd like to buy.	1	2	3	4	5
4. My car makes me feel good about myself.	1	2	3	4	5
5. I find my self-worth is tied to how my home looks.	1	2	3	4	5
6. I have a long list of things I wish I could buy.	1	2	3	4	5
7. I find myself using up a great deal of emotional and mental energy finding or thinking of things I'd like to buy.	1	2	3	4	5
8. My kids are preoccupied with things they want.	1	2	3	4	5
9. My closet is full of nice clothes that I don't wear because they're out of style.	1	2	3	4	5
10. We would give more to church or charities if we could control our spending better.	1	2	3	4	5

	Strongly Disagree	Disagree	Undecided	Agree	Strongly Agree
11. Husbands: I would be willing for my wife to stay at home with our children if it didn't mean a significant drop in our income.	1	2	3	4	5
Wives: I would be willing to stay at home with our children if it didn't mean a significant drop in our income.	1	2	3	4	5
12. We would be in full-time ministry if it didn't involve a sacrificial life-style.	1	2	3	4	5
13. Other people's opinions of my life-style matter a lot to me.	1	2	3	4	5

III. REDUCING THE PRESSURE OF MATERIALISM

(15-20 minutes)

A. Take a healthy inventory of your present life-style, with a particular emphasis on your values and attitudes toward materialism.

1. Discuss the "self-appraisal" exercise you worked on during the **Construction** time. In what one or two areas are you more materialistic than you wish you were?

▶ **1.**

TIP: *It will be up to you as leader to encourage the couples to share here. They don't need to reveal all their problems, but most people should be able to talk about a few areas where they need to think about their attitudes. If you noticed any couples chuckling as they worked on the **Construction** exercise, capitalize on that feeling by making some admissions about yourself. Or state, "I noticed a few of you making faces (or chuckling) as you filled out the self-appraisal. Did it hit close to home in any way?" Be aware that for some it may not be funny at all, but convicting. Don't dump on them, but encourage sharing.*

2. What are common ways that you rationalize materialistic attitudes?

▶ **2.**

*H*OMEBUILDERS *P*RINCIPLE

Couples need to be honest
with each other about the
influence of materialism in
their lives.

5

B. Continue growing in your understanding of the biblical perspective toward money and possessions.

1. Read Matthew 6:33. How can you practically apply this principle when making financial decisions?

▶ **1.**

ANSWER: *In the midst of making financial decisions, ask yourself questions like, "What would please God?" or, "Which choice would reflect a desire to seek His kingdom and His righteousness?" Also, be willing to act upon your convictions as you answer those questions. If you sense that a certain purchase, for example, would not please God, be willing to put aside your own desires and obey Him.*

TIP: *This is an important concept for your group members to understand. If your group members are not being practical enough, have them picture some actual decisions they might find themselves making during the next few months, and ask them if they've ever asked themselves how their decision would please God: "Let's say that you're at a department store looking at some new clothes that you'd like to buy. Have you ever asked yourself, 'How would this purchase please God?' in a situation like that? If you did, what would be some of the factors that you'd consider as you answered the question?"*

2. What practical advice can you glean from 1 Timothy 6:6-12 (especially verses 11 and 12) that would help you avoid materialism's grip?

▶ **2.**

ANSWER: *Ask yourself if you are seeking contentment in what you obtain. Flee from materialistic desires. Pursue the things of God: faith, love, godliness, etc.*

TIP: Encourage couples to be practical in their solutions.

HOMEBUILDERS PRINCIPLE

Couples need to seek contentment within the means which God has provided.

6

C. Make value-driven decisions together as a couple.

1. How can determining what true success means in life help in conquering materialism?

1.

ANSWER: If you measure success by the quality of your relationships with God and with others, you will not be as concerned with the things you own and with the comfort of your life-style.

2. Share some ideas that have worked to help you communicate together and make value-driven decisions as a couple on financial matters.

2.

TIP: Here's an optional activity: "Share, if appropriate, your own frequency and method of discussing money together as a couple." Or ask, "How do you evaluate values and stay on track?"

3. What is one thing you need to do as a couple to work together and reduce pressure from materialism?

▶ **3.**

IV. CONCLUSION

(5 minutes)

A key to making good decisions that will reduce the pressures you feel about your financial situation is simply to be honest with yourself. Here are a few questions you can use when making financial decisions:

• Am I seeking contentment in this purchase?

• Is this a need or a want?

• Have we prayed about this purchase and discussed it as a couple?

• Will the purchase please God?

• Will it create additional pressure over the next one to five years?

• Will it cause us to go into debt?

• Will our family relationships suffer because of this decision?

*Ask everyone to look at the **Make a Date** section of the personal study guide and to take a moment to agree with their mate on a time this week to complete the **HomeBuilders Project**. Remind them that at the next session you will ask them to share one experience from this interaction.*

Set a date with your mate to meet in the next few days to complete **HomeBuilders Project #2**. Your leader will ask at the next session for you to share one thing from this experience.

Date	Time	Location

Recommended Reading

Master Your Money, by Ron Blue.

In *Master Your Money*, popular financial counselor Ron Blue has combined the Bible's timeless teaching on stewardship and responsibility with the most modern insights on financial management and cash control. With detailed charts, worksheets and a handy glossary of money terms, this is the money book that you've been waiting for.

Mastering Money in Your Marriage, by Ron Blue.

One of the studies in The HomeBuilders Couples Series™, this study is designed to make money matters a tool for growth instead of a bone of contention in your marriage.

Dismiss in prayer, or invite group members to volunteer one-sentence prayers asking God's help in breaking free from the pressure of materialism in their marriages.

Invite everyone to enjoy a time of refreshments and fellowship.

INDIVIDUALLY: 30 MINUTES

1. Review the **Blueprints** questions and your responses to the **Construction** project. Write down any issues you want to discuss with your mate.

2. How would you honestly rate your success as a couple in resisting materialism and its pressures, and why?

1	2	3	4	5	6	7	8	9	10
POOR				AVERAGE					EXCELLENT
"We caved in our values to the pressures."									"We are immovable— firmly in place."

3. (Answer if applicable.) How would you evaluate your success as parents in raising children who know how to resist materialism and its pressures? Why?

1	2	3	4	5	6	7	8	9	10
POOR				AVERAGE					EXCELLENT

4. What decisions from the past are causing pressure today on you and your mate? Are there any decisions you can make today that would reduce the pressure?

5. Reread Matthew 6:33 and 1 Timothy 6:6-12. Is there anything God seems to be saying to you or your family through these passages?

6. How can you as a couple work together to reduce future pressure from materialism in your lives?

7. If you can, write down a single action point which, if you began implementing it, could really begin to make a difference in reducing pressure in your marriage and family.

1. Share your answers from the individual portion of this project.

2. List together some specific steps you can take as a couple to reduce the pressure of materialism in your financial decisions.

3. Are there any specific decisions you need to make about finances right now? Look back over the decision-making process outlined in Session One and the principles for reducing the pressure of materialism from Session Two. Evaluate the steps you need to take to make a wise decision in this area.

4. Close your time together with prayer, asking God for the wisdom and strength to make sound decisions about your finances.

Remember to bring your calendar to the next session so you can **Make a Date.**

THE PRESSURE OF WEARINESS

OBJECTIVES

In this session you will lead your group to:

■ Discuss how weariness affects their marriages;

■ Learn how going through life without a clear sense of purpose makes one weary;

■ Look at whether they are using their Sundays as rest days;

■ Examine the burden of unconfessed sin; and

■ Discuss what decisions they could make to release some of the activities, responsibilities and commitments that cause weariness.

OVERALL COMMENTS

An inevitable result of the pressures we feel is weariness. This session talks about the factors that cause weariness, but it puts the greatest emphasis on what we can do to reduce our weariness: refocusing, repenting and releasing. Your group members may gain some new perspectives on what they need to do to cure the weariness they live with from day to day.

Focus

The weariness that often plagues a marriage may have less to do with the amount of work and activities a couple is involved with and more to do with a lack of the right kind of rest.

Warm-Up

(10-15 minutes)

COMMENTS: *These questions provide the prima-ry opportunity for people to talk about their busy life-styles—what they do each day, what makes them busy, the difficulty of juggling work, church and family responsibilities, etc. These questions should spark some good discussion, because most couples feel weariness of some type. After the*

Warm Up, they'll focus more on the cures for weariness.

1. When was the last time you felt well-rested and energetic?

▶ **1.** _____

_____

2. What factors contributed to that sense of well-being? Explain.

▶ **2.** _____

_____

_____

_____

3. How would you personally assess your feelings about the pace of your life-style? Circle two of the listed words that most nearly describe you right now.

Share your two choices with the group. Tell why you picked them.

▶ **3.**

Discouraged	Cruising
Relaxed	Ragged
Exhausted	Disorganized
Organized	Adjusting
Hopeful	Encouraged
Energetic	Worthless
Out of control	Tired
Peaceful	Pressured
Panicky	Strung Out

1. The Problem of Weariness in Your Marriage

(10-15 minutes)

COMMENTS: *The three questions in this section are critical because this is where your group members talk specifically about how weariness affects marriage. It will be important for you to encourage them to be honest and open, and be prepared with answers of your own if you need to help focus the conversation.*

Weariness. It's a pressure that seems to afflict a great many marriages today. *Tired, burned out, exhausted, spent*—these words are all too familiar in our highly mobile, fast-paced society. Of course, some of our fatigue is both understandable and unavoidable. But other weariness pressures result from our choices.

A. How can you tell when your mate is weary?

What are the warning signs?

A.

B. In what ways do you think weariness has affected the quality of your marriage?

▶ **B.**

C. What habits or routines have you established as a couple to protect your marriage from burnout?

▶ **C.**

II. THREE SURPRISING CURES FOR WEARINESS

(30-45 minutes)

A. Rest Stop #1: Refocusing

Few things are as exhausting as racing through life without a clear sense of purpose and direction. To feel pulled by a packed schedule can be tiring. But to feel an absence of real purpose in all that activity can expand a natural sense of weariness into an unnatural, soul-numbing exhaustion.

1. Why is living life without a clear sense of purpose and direction so fatiguing?

▶ **1.**

ANSWER: *With no clear sense of purpose and direction, life has little meaning. You rush from one activity to another, and you end up feeling that you're just filling time instead of accomplishing something important. A sense of purpose energizes the activities in your life.*

TIP: If your group members don't seem to grasp the concept, you might want to have them recall what life was like before they received Christ. Those who became Christians as adults could remember their lack of purpose in life, their feeling of lostness. This is similar to what happens to us as we live our lives now.

We need to take time to make sense out of all that is happening to us. This is what "refocusing" means. Refocusing pumps meaning and direction back into a person's and a couple's activity by providing the time to ask basic questions like:

• Why are we driving ourselves like this?
• Where is all this taking us?
• What impact does all this activity have on our marriage? My mate?
• Is God pleased with the things we are involved in?
• Can I let anything go?

2. When was the last time, in an unhurried atmosphere, you and your mate challenged each other's schedules with questions like these?

▶ **2.**

TIP: If you've ever done this, tell about it to get the group started. Talk about where you did this— that's important, because often we are unable to have conversations like these in the normal circumstances of life at home.

*H*OMEBUILDERS *P*RINCIPLE

Nothing is as wearisome as wandering through life.

7

3. Read "a day in the life of Jesus" as found in Mark 1:21-38.

a. What were some of the pressing demands Jesus faced during this day?

▶ **a.**

ANSWER: *Continuously teaching (v. 21), rebuking (v. 25), controversy (v. 27), appointments (v. 29), healing and spiritual warfare (vv. 32,34), being in constant demand (v. 33).*

b. How did Jesus catch His breath and refocus His direction in the midst of so much stimulation and pressure? (See also Luke 4:42-43.)

▶ **b.**

ANSWER: *He got off by Himself to think, pray and take stock concerning all that was happening to Him and what it meant.*

TIP: *Again, be prepared to share something you've done to refocus direction in your marriage.*

c. In stressful and hurried times, what methods do you as a couple use to gain perspective together and refocus direction in your marriage?

▶ **c.**

Construction

(to be completed as a couple)
(10-15 minutes)

1. Look back at your answers to the **Warm Up** questions. Do you agree with how your mate answered the questions?

▶ **1.**

2. At what point in your regular weekly schedule do you normally take a "time out" to reflect upon and evaluate your activity?

▶ **2.**

3. If there is not a "time out" already in place, what could you do to create one?

▶ **3.**

4. What did Jesus mean when He said, "The Sabbath was made for man" (Mark 2:27)? "Made for man" to do what?

▶ **4.**

5. What role does Sunday play in your weekly schedule? Check one:

5. ❑ It's a day like any other day.
❑ It's a day to "catch up."
❑ It's a day to relax.
❑ It's a day for recreation.
❑ It's a day to worship and evaluate.
❑ Other_____

Why do think Sunday is treated this way?

6. What steps could we take to make Sunday a more meaningful "rest day" and a cure from the exhaustion of unclear living and purposeless activity?

6.

7. Read Isaiah 40:28-31 together. How does this passage apply to taking a weekly "time out"?

7.

Blueprints

TIP: If there is time, have couples share what they said about Sundays during the **Construction** *project.*

B. Rest Stop #2: Repentance

1. It may at first seem odd that repentance can be coupled with rest. And yet, according to Jeremiah 9:2-5, what is the source of Israel's weariness?

▶ **1.**

ANSWER: *Adultery, treachery, lying, desire, deceit, slander—all activities that require repentance. Sin wearies us!*

2. How did David express this same sense of exhaustion in Psalm 32:3,4?

▶ **2.**

ANSWER: *He tried to conceal his sin, and his body "wasted away." He groaned. He felt the heavy conviction of God on him, and this robbed him of his strength.*

3. According to Psalm 32:5, how did David get relief from his weariness?

▶ **3.**

ANSWER: *He acknowledged his sin to God. He made it known. He stopped ignoring it and fighting to conceal it.*

4. What are some ways that people expend great amounts of time and energy seeking to conceal or make excuses for sinful behaviors in a marriage? (Avoid pointing fingers on this one!)

▶ **4.**

ANSWER: *They blame others. They lie. They try to keep their mates from discovering their sin.*

TIP: *If your group members are answering this question too generally, make it more specific: "How do people try to conceal or cover their sin in the area of finances or in sexual morality?"*

5. Read Psalm 32:3-5 and James 5:15,16. What cure for weariness do these passages offer?

▶ **5.**

ANSWER: *A person who confesses his or her sins can be forgiven and healed.*

HOMEBUILDERS PRINCIPLE

Unacknowledged sin has a price: Exhaustion! Real rest is found in a clear conscience.

8

6. In what ways has humble confession been a pain and energy saver for you and for your marriage?

▶ **6.**

TIP: *It's important for your group members to realize just what type of burden we carry upon our-*

selves by not confessing our sins. If discussion on these questions has been short, be sure to share an example from your own life when you confessed a sin that was burdening you. Or refer them back to when they received Christ: "In what ways did you experience healing and relief when you confessed your sins and received Christ as your Savior?"

C. Rest Stop #3: Releasing

To release things that seem important and feel important but are really not can bring an almost instant refreshment.

1. Read Luke 10:38-42. How does Jesus sum up much of Martha's weariness? What words does He use?

▶ **1.** _____

ANSWER: *She was worried and bothered by "so many things."*

2. What kinds of avoidable pressures was Jesus trying to get Martha to release?

▶ **2.** _____

ANSWER: *He wanted her to see that she was putting pressure on herself by being so busy with preparations and serving. She was being driven by her own self-imposed agenda.*

3. How does He help her get a more accurate perspective?

▶ **3.** _____

ANSWER: *By helping her see that only a few things are really vital—everything else is really optional.*

4. What are some past activities and concerns that have exhausted both your life and marriage and that you now know were really unnecessary?

▶ **4.**

HOMEBUILDERS PRINCIPLE

In some areas of life, letting go may be the best strategy. Couples can decrease pressure in their lives by deciding to cut down on their responsibilities, expectations and commitments.

9

5. What are some decisions you could make to decrease current responsibilities, expectations or commitments that weigh you down? (Your honesty here may help other couples escape the tyranny of doing unnecessary things.)

▶ **5.**

III. SUMMARY

It is clear that every marriage is pressured by weariness. But avoidable weariness can rob a couple of the life and energy their marriage was meant to enjoy. As we have seen, such weariness is not solved by taking a "few days off"; the solutions are usually much more subtle. Refocusing, repentance and releasing unnecessary activities and concerns are three ways of thinking more deeply about our exhaustion and finding real cures for weariness.

*Ask everyone to look at the **Make a Date** section of the personal study guide and to take a moment to agree with their mate on a time this week to complete the **HomeBuilders Project**. Remind them that at the next session you will ask them to share one experience from this interaction.*

Set a date with your mate to meet in the next few days to complete **HomeBuilders Project #3.** Your leader will ask at the next session for you to share one thing from this experience.

Date	Time	Location

Recommended Reading

Call attention to the **Recommended Reading.**

Little House on the Freeway, by Tim Kimmel.

Tim Kimmel has his finger on the pulse of American culture. Yet he offers more than a rehash of the pain and problems. This book is a storehouse of practical counsel from a man who speaks to thousands of families each year.

Dismiss in prayer, or invite group members to volunteer one-sentence prayers asking God's help in handling the pressure of weariness in their marriages.

Invite everyone to enjoy a time of refreshments and fellowship.

HomeBuilders Project #3

This project has three parts: One individual section and two to be completed as a couple. Each person should bring to their meeting a calendar that covers the next two months.

INDIVIDUALLY: 20-30 MINUTES

1. Review *Rest Stop #2*. Reread the Scriptures recommended there. Think back on the group discussion.

2. Read Psalm 139:23-24. Does this statement by David express the desire of your own heart? If so, ask God honestly, "What sin am I not facing up to that is wearing me out?" Sit in silence before Him and list below those answers that surface in your conscience.

_____

_____

_____

_____

_____

_____

_____

_____

_____

_____

_____

_____

3. Now read 1 John 1:9. Do you believe this statement? If so . . .

Confess to God right now what you have recorded in the space above. Tell Him each item specifically. Admit that these things are wrong and that you want to change.

Now thank God that He has forgiven you for these wrongdoings. Before God . . . you are now forgiven! Clean!

As a gesture of your faith, draw an X across the sins you listed above. Then write the word *forgiven*.

As a final symbolic gesture of this great truth, tear this page out of the book. Destroy it and throw it away. Because of your confession, God no longer holds these sins against you. Rejoice and be thankful!

Close this time in prayer, asking God's help in those areas where you have previously failed. You might also determine now to seek the counsel and help of others to address the weaknesses of your life.

INTERACT AS A COUPLE: 45-60 MINUTES

1. Review together Rest Stop #3.

2. Using a pencil (so you can erase!), write down on your calendar all the major events and activities that will consume your time over the next two months. Also write in habitual items and regular meetings that you may not think of as "events" (choir practice, your daily run, etc.).

3. Now fill out the following chart together. Be sure to listen to one another. Often your mate can see what is unnecessary in your life better than you can.

Unnecessary things we can let go of:

Unnecessary things in _____'s life (fill in name):

Unnecessary things in _____'s life (fill in name):

Unnecessary things we do together:

4. What are the action steps you must take together to let go of unnecessary activities and commitments in your life together?

_____

_____

_____

_____

5. What are the conflicts that surface between you as you ask these questions? List them below.

_____

_____

_____

6. Seek to resolve these differences with mutual understanding and love.

7. Commit to "refocus" again in six weeks. Remember: Nothing is as wearisome as wandering through life!

8. Close in prayer.

Remember to bring your calendar to
the next session so you can **Make a Date.**

SEASONAL PRESSURES

OBJECTIVES

In this session you will lead your group members as they:

- Discuss the pressures that come with each "season" that a typical marriage passes through;
- Learn about the critical need for advance preparation as each new season approaches; and
- Share some practical ways they learned to decrease the pressure they felt during the seasons they have already experienced.

OVERALL COMMENTS

1. Every couple is working through some stage of their married life, and nearly every couple is unprepared in at least some ways for what they face in that stage. It's easy for them to let that pressure overwhelm them. Also, it's easy for them to feel isolated, as if nobody else is going through the same struggles. This session is designed for couples to encourage each other during their seasons of life.

2. This session has a greater emphasis than others on couples sharing with others; you'll notice less Scripture and more discussion questions. Your session will succeed if you

are able to create an environment where couples are free to share what they are struggling with at this stage in their lives, and are free to encourage others with what has helped them cope.

3. Remember the theme of the study: how our decisions affect the pressure we feel in our marriages. This is important to understand as you discuss the "seasons of marriage," because our decisions on a daily basis play a large role in how we adjust to new responsibilities and new circumstances.

Every marriage will pass through special "seasons" that present specific and unique challenges. A wise couple will prepare for each.

Warm-Up

(10-15 minutes)

1. What kind of preparation (counseling, advice, etc.), if any, did you receive before marriage?

▶**1.**

2. What benefits did this premarital preparation bring to the opening years of your marriage?

▶**2.**

3. Whether you had any premarital preparation or not, looking back now, what kinds of issues would you have liked to have been prepared for as you started your marriage?

▶**3.**

I. An Overall Perspective on Marital "Seasons"

(10-15 minutes)

Every marriage goes through a series of distinct phases or "seasons." By "season," we mean a specific time period in which certain events, issues, adjustments and needs are typical and clearly different from those associated with other periods of the marriage.

Most people recognize that their lives proceed in recognizable stages—for example, the teenage years, young adulthood, middle age, and so forth. Marriages, too, have their distinct phases, and each one is like a marriage within a marriage. Every season requires fresh perspectives, new commitments and a special kind of preparation from each marriage partner to successfully walk through it.

The problem is that many couples are not prepared for the pressures they will face when they enter a new season in their marriages. In the same way that many couples begin marriage with little idea of what faces them, many begin each season of their married lives with little thought or understanding of what lies ahead.

A. What "season" do you think your marriage is in right now? What seasons has it passed through?

► **A.**

TIP: *This is a question that every couple should be able to answer. Later in this session you'll work through more specific definitions of different seasons, but each person should be able to identify roughly where they are now: newly married, young parents, etc.*

B. What events or adjustments indicated that a new season of married life had arrived for you?

► **B.**

C. How can the coming of a new marital season bring added pressure and stress to a marriage?

► **C.**

ANSWER: *Couples are not prepared for the new responsibilities and adjustments. They often don't make the kinds of decisions that could relieve some of the pressure they feel.*

Just as many couples do not receive adequate marriage preparation during their engagement, they also receive inadequate instruction for new seasons of life that they enter. As a result, it's easy to be surprised and even overwhelmed by the unique pressures they feel.

ℋOMEBUILDERS 𝒫RINCIPLE

Advance preparation is the best
pressure-release value for a
new marital season.

10

II. THE PITFALLS OF SEASONAL PRESSURE

CASE STUDY

(15-20 minutes)

Larry and Jackie would say that the first five years of their marriage were excellent. During that time, Larry settled into a well-paying job while Jackie taught elementary school. They were able to purchase a comfortable three-bedroom home that, even now, meets their needs.

Recently, Larry and Jackie celebrated their ninth anniversary, but with little joy. Their marriage feels different now. Two years ago, Jackie left teaching after having her second child. She enjoys being at home with her children, but sometimes she feels starved for adult conversation. And she doesn't feel she is accomplishing as much with her life as she once did.

Larry has had a major change, too. Since his promotion to regional manager, he is traveling much more, and he often works longer hours. Larry also continues to play basketball every weekend and, though Jackie complains, Larry feels he deserves some time off.

Jackie feels Larry is not nearly involved enough with her and the children. Larry, on the other hand, feels he is competing with the kids more and more for Jackie's affection.

Both Larry and Jackie are feeling a growing isolation between one another. They're surprised at the sudden flashes of anger they have felt toward one another. Their excellent marriage has turned sour. As their resentment builds, they are frightened to think they may be falling out of love.

A. How would you summarize this couple's problem? What has clearly changed in their marriage, whether they know it or not?

▶ **A.**

ANSWER: *They are facing many of the typical pressures of a couple with a growing family and a growing occupation. There is now a major issue as never before. Spontaneity is decreasing and personal needs are increasing. Those pressures can pull a couple apart or drive them together, depending on how they react and adjust to them.*

B. How would you advise Larry and Jackie? What adjustments are needed in this new season of their life together? What new commitments would you say they will need to make to one another to recapture the success they enjoyed in the opening five years of their marriage?

▶ **B.**

ANSWER: *Jackie needs a different outlook on her present role. She needs encouragement—primarily from Larry—that staying home to raise the children during these early years is vitally important. At the same time, she needs the freedom to get out of the home to be involved in other people's lives as well. Larry, meanwhile, needs to take a hard look at his schedule. Does he really need to be working* as many hours at the office as he is now? Can he switch to another job that would allow him to be at home more? At the very least, he may need to take a hard look at whether he really needs to be playing basketball on Saturdays. During this season of life, it may not be best for his marriage and his family. Larry and Jackie both need to carve out time to work on their relationship. There are some pressures they can't avoid; they can't give up their children, for example. But they can lessen the pressure by making their relationship a greater priority.

TIP: *This is where the conversation should begin to get personal. Encourage couples to share what has worked for them at the same stage. Ask questions like, "Can any of you relate to what Larry and Jackie are going through?"*

III. The Seasons of Marriage

(20-30 minutes)

In some ways, marriage seasons are not difficult to determine. And yet it may not be that easy to recognize the distinct pressures of each and what adjustments must be made to counter such pressures. At any rate, the better a couple can prepare for a marital season, the more advantages that couple will have as they try to manage the unique pressures that season brings with it.

A. How can you apply the following verses to the principle of understanding different seasons of marriage and preparing for them in advance?

▶ **A.**

TIP: *If any group members have not talked much, assign verses to them to read, and have them answer the question: "John, why don't you read*

Luke 14:28-30 and tell how you think it applies to understanding different seasons of marriage and preparing for them?"

1. Luke 14:28-30   ▶ **1.** _____

ANSWER: *We need to plan ahead and "calculate the cost" as we enter new seasons of life and marriage. This means taking an honest look at the pressures and trials we're likely to face.*

2. Proverbs 24:3,4   ▶ **2.** _____

ANSWER: *We need to seek God's wisdom as we build our marital "houses." And we need to be willing to follow His guidance rather than our own desires.*

B. On the following pages is a chart showing the seasons that most marriages move through, along with typical, pressing issues that couples face in each season. As you read through these and discuss them, feel free to add any other issues that you feel are relevant.

TIP: *If you have time, spend a few moments on the "seasons" represented in your group. Refer to your earlier discussion about the seasons that your group members have passed through and ask, "Are there any other issues you would add to this list, based on our earlier discussion?"*

SEASON	PRESSING ISSUES
NEWLY MARRIED	Defining and agreeing on your new roles as "husband" and "wife"—who does what? Developing a relationship with in-laws. Learning how to get along on a daily basis. Learning how to communicate and resolve conflict. Adjusting to differences: values, tastes, needs, etc. Other:____
DIRECTION FOR MARRIED LIFE— MARRIED WITH PRESCHOOLERS	Making major decisions concerning careers and children. Maintaining time for one another and not losing touch. Developing new roles and accepting new responsibilities as you begin raising children. Handling the growing money squeeze. Keeping the relationship fresh. Coping with growing responsibilities at work. Other:____

SEASON	PRESSING ISSUES
GROWING MARRIAGE—SCHOOL-AGED FAMILY	Juggling the pace of your expanding responsibilities in life. Maintaining sanity in your schedule as your children begin school, add new friends, and begin activities of their own (sports, music lessons, Girl Scouts, etc.). Handling the growing money squeeze with savings, college, retirement concerns. Adjusting to teenagers. Keeping romance alive after 10-20 years of marriage. Other:_____
MATURE MARRIED LIFE—LAUNCHING AND RELEASING FAMILY	Mid-life crises. Dealing with aging and ill parents. Increasing health concerns. Money pressures with children in college. Releasing children successfully into the adult world. Other:_____
MARRIAGE IN TRANSITION—EMPTY NEST	New roles for both husband and wife after children. Refocusing on the marriage relationship. Developing a new life-style. Allocating resources for future needs. Changing relationship with

SEASON	PRESSING ISSUES
	children as they marry and begin families of their own. Defining roles as "in-laws" and "grandparents." Other: _____
MARRIAGE IN RETIREMENT	Dealing with health setbacks. Finding new purpose after work. Adjusting to retirement income. Other: _____

C. From the outline of marriage seasons just presented, which seasons do the couples in your group fall into? List them.

D. Share what has helped you the most in handling the season of life you are now in (or a season you've passed through). What adjustments, insights, books, etc. have helped take some of the pressure off your marriage in certain seasons?

► **C.** _____

_____

_____

_____

► **D.** _____

_____

_____

_____

TIP: *This question and the next two are the most important of the session. This is where your couples can help and encourage each other in facing the current "seasonal" pressures they are facing. Ask older couples to tell what helped them when they were going through an earlier season of their marriage. Spend as much time as possible on this section.*

E. If you can, share a Scripture passage you have found especially relevant and helpful when applied to a particular season of your marriage.

F. In what ways could you be preparing now for the next season of your married life? Discuss.

▶ **E.**

▶ **F.**

IV. Summary

In Ephesians 5:15, Paul exhorts us, "Be careful how you walk, not as unwise men, but as wise." As we have seen in this session, such wisdom is acquired in part by first seeking to understand the issues we will face, then preparing for them. A wise couple not only knows that their marriage will move through distinct phases of change—seasons—they also do what they can to make themselves ready for each.

Construction

(to be completed as a couple)
(5-10 minutes)

1. What one point from the group discussion stands out in your mind as applying powerfully to your marriage?

▶ **1.**

2. What one insight or resource can you draw upon right now to help you address the marriage season in which you find yourselves?

▶ **2.**

Make a Date

*Ask everyone to look at the **Make a Date** section of the personal study guide and to take a moment to agree with their mate on a time this week to complete the **HomeBuilders Project**. Point out that this week's format is a little different from that of the previous weeks; they will meet together first, separate to work individually, then come together to complete the project. Remind them that at the next session you will ask them to share one experience from this interaction.*

Set a date with your mate to meet in the next few days to complete **HomeBuilders Project #4**. Your leader will ask at the next session for you to share one thing from this experience.

Date	Time	Location

Recommended Reading

Call attention to the **Recommended Reading***.*

Love for a Lifetime, by James Dobson.

This is a keepsake book every married or engaged couple should read together. Dr. Dobson offers wisdom, counsel and an impassioned challenge to keep love alive for the rest of your life.

Seasons of a Marriage, by H. Norman Wright.

After identifying three basic reasons why marriages dissolve, author and counselor H. Norman Wright attempts to prepare people for the typical changes that they will encounter in married life. In this book couples of all ages will discover the different stages of marriage that they will encounter, and how to prepare for the challenges they never thought about during their courtship period.

Dismiss in prayer, or invite group members to volunteer one-sentence prayers asking God's help in walking through the seasons of their marriages.

Invite everyone to enjoy a time of refreshments and fellowship.

HomeBuilders Project #4

INTERACT AS A COUPLE: 30-45 MINUTES

1. In what areas do you feel you need the most help during your current marriage season?

2. What resources can you draw upon right now to help you walk through this marriage season? What preparation can you do for those pressures just ahead?

3. Make a list of couples you know who have successfully completed the marital season you are now in. Consider setting a date with one of these couples for the purpose of interviewing them on how they did it. If you agree to do this, plan specifically. Which one of you will take the responsibility to call the other couple?

4. Discuss together the commitments you will have to make and the responsibilities you will have to assume in order to be successful in the particular marriage season you are now facing. Be specific and listen carefully to your mate. Avoid pointing your finger or blaming! Instead, work for mutual understanding. List the insights you receive in the space below.

INDIVIDUALLY: 30-45 MINUTES

Exchange personal study guides. In the space provided in **HomeBuilders Project #4** (in your mate's book), compose a set of "New Marriage Vows." Turn the commitments and responsibilities you discussed above into personal promises of love and commitment to your mate for the particular season you are facing in your marriage. Be sure to include new expressions of love and appreciation!

My New Marriage Vows

INTERACT AS A COUPLE: 25 MINUTES

Come back together and read your new marriage vows to your mate as an expression of fresh commitment to your marriage. Remember: Every marriage season needs new vows and fresh commitments. Return your personal study guides to one another and close this session in prayer.

NOTE: You might consider giving these vows publicly before others to make these commitments even more significant.

Remember to bring your calendar to the next session so you can **Make a Date.**

TAKING THE PRESSURE OFF SEX

(MEN'S SESSION)

OBJECTIVES

You will help your group members look at ways to improve their sexual relationships with their wives as they:

- Discuss the pressures that affect the sexual relationship;
- Look at the priority of sex in marriage;
- Seek to understand the differences between men and women in this area; and
- Discuss how they can sacrificially meet their wives' needs.

OVERALL COMMENTS

1. Many couples report that they feel pressure in their sexual relationship and experience intense frustration as a result. At the same time, this aspect of marriage is not always easy for people to talk about, especially men. That's why you're splitting the husbands and wives into separate groups for this session— to encourage more open discussion.

2. Your job as leader will be to create an environment where the men are able to loosen up a little and talk more freely than they normally do. This doesn't mean they should share a lot of intimate details—there is a warning about this just before the **Warm Up**. But your willingness to talk about your marriage and the pressures you feel in the sexual relationship will be crucial in helping the men relax and talk.

3. Important note: This session does not deal with sensitive areas such as sexual abuse, impotence or dysfunction. However, problems such as these may surface during your discussion. Depending on the situation, and how your group responds, this could offer a great opportunity for you to minister to each other. At the same time, watch to see whether the discussion is becoming too sidetracked, and whether you and the group are capable of helping this person meaningfully at this time. If you sense that you need to let the session continue as originally planned, you could stop the discussion at an appropriate point and spend some time in group prayer before moving on. Then approach the person after the session and offer to meet with him personally—or recommend a counselor.

Understanding your
mate's needs and
sacrificially acting to
meet them is essential to
a mutually rewarding
sex life in marriage.

(10-15 minutes)

IMPORTANT NOTE: *In this session we are going
to discuss a very delicate area of marital life. It is
important that each person share only what he feels
comfortable in sharing. Remember that this is the
most intimate area of a marriage relationship and
must be spoken of with dignity. Share nothing that
may embarrass your wife later. Use this time to
encourage one another in this all-important area of
a marriage.*

1. How would you describe the perfect romantic evening?

2. How do you think your wife would describe the perfect romantic evening?

3. In our research for this study, we found that many Christian men are uncomfortable talking with others about the sexual dimension of marriage. Why do you think this is truer for men than for women?

▶**1.** _____

▶**2.** _____

TIP: *Since the wives are answering these same questions, you could add a twist for this* **Warm Up**: *Have someone in each group take notes on the answers given for questions one and two. Then exchange these notes and let each group see how the other answered the questions.*

▶**3.** _____

ANSWERS: *The process of sexual intercourse is far riskier for a man than it is for a woman. He is often the initiator, while she is the responder. Also, a man's self-esteem is often more tightly bound with his sexual identity. So he may be more uncomfortable talking with other men about it. In addition, we live in a society where sex is often the subject of jokes and bravado. Men who grew up talking and joking and bragging about sex often decide to change their habits once they become Christians. They go from one extreme to the other, and avoid discussing it completely.*

TIP: *Be sure to get the men to answer this question, because it could be an ice-breaker. By getting them to talk about why it may be uncomfortable for them to talk about sex, you should loosen them up!*

1. How Pressure Affects the Sexual Relationship

CASE STUDY

(15-20 minutes)

Reid and Susan struggled to keep their passion in check during their courtship and engagement. They were both Christians and were committed to purity, and they experienced the fruits of that commitment after they were married. During their first three years they enjoyed a regular sexual relationship that was satisfying to both of them.

But things began to change after they had two children within two years. Here is a typical day for Reid and Susan now, during their seventh year of marriage:

6:00-7:15 A.M.: Wake up, eat, prepare for work, feed and dress the kids.

7:15-8:00 A.M.: Reid leaves for his 30-minute drive to his job at a bank; Susan drops off one child at day-care and another at preschool, then drives 15 minutes to the hospital where she works as a nurse.

6:00 P.M.: Susan arrives home exhausted after picking up kids and shopping for groceries; she starts getting dinner ready.

6:30 P.M.: Reid arrives home with a glazed look in his eyes.

6:30-7:00 P.M.: Dinner, clean kitchen.

7:00-8:30 P.M.: Take care of kids—games, baths, bedtime.

8:30-10:00 or 11:00 P.M.: Television, phone calls, catching up on unfinished work, paying bills, etc.

10:00 or 11:00 P.M.: Bedtime.

Reid and Susan feel that their life-style is too hectic, but they don't know how to change it. It seems they hardly ever get a chance to spend time together the way they used to. Once they finally get the kids to sleep and other responsibilities taken care of, all they feel like doing is watching television or sleeping.

Both Reid and Susan are frustrated with their sex life. Reid can't understand why Susan doesn't want to make love as much as she used to. Susan feels pressure to have sex more often than she wants. She resents Reid's sex drive and wonders how he can just jump into bed and start making love when they have hardly talked to each other for days.

On top of that, Susan has had trouble losing weight after bearing two children. She doesn't feel pretty, and she feels hurt when Reid makes remarks about "losing that flab." And Reid doesn't feel as attracted to Susan anymore. Other wives lose their post-baby weight and keep their good looks, so why can't Susan? At the same time, Reid isn't as trim as he used to be, either, though Susan hesitates to say anything about it.

The irony is that both Reid and Susan are still interested in sex. But they have drifted apart; the romance is gone. It seems the only time they can get together is during the weekend, and not always then.

A. What are the main pressures and problems that Reid and Susan are experiencing?

▶**A.**

ANSWER: *They have an extremely busy schedule, with both partners working. When they have any time to focus on each other, they are usually exhausted. What time they do have is often spent watching television. They don't understand each other's needs in the sexual area. They are too concerned with outward appearance.*

B. How can misunderstanding your mate's needs create pressure in your marriage and in the sexual dimension of your relationship?

▶**B.**

ANSWER: *It's easy to forget that your mate's needs are usually different from yours. It causes frustration when you expect your mate to feel or act the same way you do. For example, a man may proceed more quickly while making love than his wife wants him to.*

C. How has a busy schedule, with its accompanying pressure and responsibility, affected your sexual relationship?

▶**C.**

TIP: *Be prepared with a specific example from your own relationship. This will help the others think of similar instances.*

D. How does stress affect men and women in this area?

D.

ANSWER: *In a general sense, stress can heighten the need for sexual release in a man. For the woman, it can heighten the need for a stronger relationship. Also, stress can easily cause conflict between a husband and wife, and when conflict occurs, the sexual relationship will suffer.*

II. THE PRIORITY OF THE SEXUAL RELATIONSHIP IN MARRIAGE

(5-10 minutes)

A. Read 1 Corinthians 7:5. What warning does this verse contain?

A.

ANSWER: *A husband and wife need to "stop depriving one another" so that Satan has no foothold to tempt them.*

B. It seems this passage tells us to be deliberate about making the sexual relationship in marriage a priority. What are some practical ways you can do this?

B.

TIP: *This question will be answered through the material in Part III of* **Blueprints**. *For now, see how your group members can answer the question. If they have trouble, ask, "Have you struggled with making sex a priority in your marriage?"*

ℋOMEBUILDERS ℘RINCIPLE

Couples need to make their sexual relationship a high priority.

11

III. How You Can Reduce Pressure in Your Sexual Relationship

(30-45 minutes)

A. Understand your wife's needs.

▶ **1.**

1. From your own experience, what is the most important lesson you have learned about how sex is different for a man and a woman?

▶ **2.** In his book, *His Needs, Her Needs,* Willard Harley lists the following needs in a marriage: admiration, affection, an attractive spouse, honesty and openness, family commitment, conversation, domestic support, recreational companionship, sexual fulfillment and financial support.

a. On the chart below, rank from 1 (most important) to 5 (least important) how you think *men* prioritized these needs. Then do the same thing for *women* on the right.

Men		Women
_____	Admiration	_____
_____	Affection	_____
_____	An attractive spouse	_____
_____	Honesty and openness	_____

Men		Women
____	Family commitment	____
____	Conversation	____
____	Domestic support	____
____	Recreational companionship	____
____	Sexual fulfillment	____
____	Financial support	____

TIP: *Have the men explain their rankings.*

b. Discuss the answers to the survey found in the group leader's guide. (Answers also can be found at the end of this session.)

ANSWER: *The top five needs for men were: 1. sexual fulfillment; 2. recreational companionship; 3. an attractive spouse; 4. domestic support; 5. admiration. The top five for women were: 1. affection; 2. conversation; 3. honesty and openness; 4. financial support; 5. family commitment.*

3. Read 1 Peter 3:7. What are some practical things you can do to give your wife honor as a woman? How can you grant her honor especially in this area of sex?

▶ **3.**

_____

_____

_____

_____

ANSWER: *You can grant her honor by courting her, by continuing to express your happiness at being her husband, by telling your children what a wonderful mother they have, by spending time with her. You can grant her honor in sex by seeking to please her.*

TIP: *Ask the group, "What is the most romantic thing you've ever done for your wife?" Encourage the men to share what they have done.*

4. What advice would you give the man who is more interested in love-making than his wife?

4.

ANSWER: *First, understand the cause: A woman's own feelings of insecurity or past rejection with her husband may affect her sex drive. Other inhibitors are pressure at work, past sexual abuse, and fear of failure. Second, discuss the problem as a couple and make adjustments in your schedule. If necessary talk to a qualified Christian counselor.*

B. Be more considerate of your mate's needs.

1. Read Ephesians 5:28,29. Practically speaking, how can a man love his wife as his own body?

1.

ANSWER: *By considering her needs to be just as important as his own. The normal person is very concerned with how his body looks and feels. This is a picture of the extent to which a man should love his wife and seek to meet her needs.*

2. Read Philippians 2:3-4. Why do you think that an unselfish attitude is essential to a mutually fulfilling sex life with your wife?

2.

ANSWER: *Wives want to be pleased just as much as husbands do in the sexual relationship. If your wife feels that you are using her to gain your own gratification, she will become resentful. You should seek to please her while making love. The irony is that most men actually receive greater sexual plea-*

sure themselves when their wives are fully aroused, and yet they sometimes forget this fact and seek only to get their own pleasure out of the act.

TIP: *If you think your group is open enough, here's an optional question: "How has selfishness had a negative impact on your marriage in the sexual area?"*

ℋOMEBUILDERS 𝒫RINCIPLE

To build true sexual intimacy, defeat selfishness by focusing on what your mate needs.

12

C. Make your relationship a priority.

1. What would your wife say are the primary activities that rob the two of you of time to spend together?

▶ **1.**

- ❏ Watching TV
- ❏ Reading
- ❏ Children
- ❏ Hobbies, sports or recreational activities
- ❏ Work
- ❏ Church activities
- ❏ Civic activities
- ❏ Other

TIP: *This is a crucial area in which to challenge your group. Many couples could spend more time cultivating their relationship if only they were committed to doing so. Television is an especially big robber of time. You might want to use this optional question: "What changes could you make in order to have more time to spend together?"*

2. Many women express a need for their husbands to share more of their lives with them. What are some practical ways you can work at being more open and honest with your wife and share more of your life with her?

▶ 2.

TIP: Again, be prepared with an example of your own.

3. Mutual trust and respect are at the core of a healthy marriage relationship. What can you do to elicit your wife's respect?

▶ 3.

4. Nonsexual, physical affection is one of the most powerful relationship builders for a woman. Share what you've learned in this area.

▶ 4.

TIP: This is an important point for men to understand, because they are often aroused so easily. It's important for men to understand that every hug and kiss does not have to lead to sexual intercourse.

5. Spiritual intimacy with your mate is essential to experiencing a full and meaningful sexual relationship. Choose one step that would most encourage your wife to respect you and share with you spiritually:

▶ **5.**

a. Read the Scriptures together daily for a month.

b. Pray with her daily about your life together, your marriage and your family.

c. Read a book together and discuss it.

d. Begin to share with your wife what God is doing in your life—what He is teaching you, burdening you about, or convicting you about in your private life.

e. Lead a new HomeBuilders Couples study in your home after this one is finished.

6. What is one change you could make in the next week to build your relationship with your wife?

▶ **6.**

D. Court your wife.

1. Think back to when you first courted your wife. What did you do to gain her attention and add romance to your relationship?

▶ **1.**

2. Why do so many men stop courting their wives after they are married?

▶ **2.**

ANSWER: *Many men lose their motivation after marriage, feeling as if the "battle is won." In reality, of course, the "battle" never stops. You need to continue courting and seeking to please her.*

3. If appropriate, share one creative idea of how you or another person you know has managed to add romance to the marriage relationship. (You may want to write down any good ideas that other group members contribute!)

▶ **3.** _____

_____

_____

Answer for Blueprints Question 2a. The top five needs for men were: 1. sexual fulfillment; 2. recreational companionship; 3. an attractive spouse; 4. domestic support; 5. admiration. The top five for women were: 1. affection; 2. conversation; 3. honesty and openness; 4. financial support; 5. family commitment.

*Ask everyone to look at the **Make a Date** section of the personal study guide and to take a moment to agree with their mate on a time this week to complete the **HomeBuilders Project**. Remind them that at the next session you will ask them to share one experience from this interaction.*

Set a date with your mate to meet in the next few days to complete **HomeBuilders Project #5**. Your leader will ask at the next session for you to share one thing from this experience.

Date	Time	Location

Recommended Reading

Call attention to the **Recommended Reading**.

Intended for Pleasure, by Ed and Gaye Wheat.

Here is a book that will bring you to a fuller awareness of the pleasures that can be found in God-directed sexual union. The Wheats apply what the Bible has to say about sex to our everyday lives in a meaningful way.

The Questions Book for Marriage Intimacy
by Dennis and Barbara Rainey.

This short book offers 31 questions you've probably never thought to ask your mate. These questions will ignite your curiosity and rekindle your fascination for each other. These questions will spark many memorable hours of sharing, sharpen your understanding of your mate and stimulate closeness in new areas of your marriage.

Dismiss in prayer, or invite group members to volunteer one-sentence prayers asking God's help in handling sexual pressures in their marriages.

Invite everyone to enjoy a time of refreshments and fellowship.

INDIVIDUALLY: 30 MINUTES

1. Complete the following exercise to judge how you and your mate handle the following aspects of your sexual relationship. Circle the number that corresponds to your answer. Draw an *X* through the number you think your mate will select.

	Low				High
The relationship we enjoy prior to lovemaking.	1	2	3	4	5
Viewing sex with positive anticipation.	1	2	3	4	5
The way you decide to have sex together.	1	2	3	4	5
The amount of communication during lovemaking (i.e. giving feedback, expressing desires, etc.).	1	2	3	4	5
Frequency of physical intimacy.	1	2	3	4	5
Gentleness and tenderness during lovemaking.	1	2	3	4	5
Variety of sexual experiences together.	1	2	3	4	5
Understanding of one another in this area.	1	2	3	4	5

2. Do you fully trust your mate with your body? If not, in what aspect do you feel distrust? Why? Refer to 1 Corinthians 7:3-5.

3. List any inaccurate attitudes you may have about your body or your mate's body. Refer to Song of Solomon 5:1-16; 7:1-9.

4. Complete the following to share later with your mate:

a. When we are sharing physical love, I like for you to...

b. It makes me feel discouraged when you...

5. What are two things you can do to decrease the pressure either or both of you may feel in your sexual relationship?

6. Look back over the points we covered during the session on sexual intimacy. What are the top three things you think would really please your mate?

7. Evaluate before God whether there is any bitterness in your heart toward your mate regarding your sexual relationship. Read 1 John 1:9 and confess any anger or resentment that may have built up toward your mate.

INTERACT AS A COUPLE: 30 MINUTES

1. Share with each other what you wrote during the individual time.

2. Choose three decisions you can make together that will improve your sexual relationship.

3. Schedule a whole day and night within the next month when the two of you can get away for a special time of communication and intimacy.

4. Pray together and thank God for each other as His provision for each other's sexual needs. Make a commitment to each other to improve communication and intimacy.

Remember to bring your calendar to the next session you can **Make a Date.**

TAKING THE PRESSURE OFF SEX

(WOMEN'S SESSION)

OBJECTIVES

You will help your group members look at ways to improve their sexual relationships with their husbands as they;

- Discuss the pressures that affect the sexual relationship;
- Look at the priority of sex in marriage;
- Seek to understand the differences between men and women in this area; and
- Discuss how they can sacrificially meet their husbands' needs.

OVERALL COMMENTS

1. Many couples report that they feel pressure in their sexual relationship and experience intense frustration as a result. At the same time, this aspect of marriage is not always easy for people to talk about. That's why you're splitting the husbands and wives into separate groups for this session—to encourage more open discussion.

2. Your job as leader will be to create an environment where the women are able to loosen up a little and talk more freely than they normally do. This doesn't mean they should share a lot of intimate details—there is a warning about this just before the **Warm Up**. But your willingness to talk about your marriage and the pressures you feel in the sexual relationship will be crucial in helping the women relax and talk.

3. Some wives feel resentment in this area because they feel their husbands are selfishly concerned only with their own pleasure. If this attitude is expressed, especially during the discussion about meeting a mate's needs, you might want to tell them briefly what the husbands are talking about in their discussion—the same thing!

4. Important note: This session does not deal with sensitive areas such as sexual abuse, impotence or dysfunction. However, problems such as these may surface during your discussion. Depending on the situation, and how your group responds, this could offer a great opportunity for you to minister to each other. At the same time, watch to see whether the discussion is becoming too sidetracked, and whether you and the group are capable of helping this person meaningfully at this time. If you sense that you need to let the session continue as originally planned, you could stop the discussion at an appropriate point and spend some time in group prayer before moving on. Then approach the person after the session and offer to meet with her personally—or recommend a counselor.

Understanding your
mate's needs and
sacrificially acting to
meet them is essential
to a mutually rewarding
sex life in marriage.

(10-15 minutes)

IMPORTANT NOTE: *In this session we are going to discuss a very delicate area of marital life. It is important that each person share only what she feels comfortable in sharing. Remember that this is the most intimate area of a marriage relationship and must be spoken of with dignity. Share nothing that may embarrass your husband later. Use this time to encourage one another in this all-important area of a marriage.*

1. How would you describe a perfect romantic evening?

▶ **1.**

2. How do you think your husband would describe the perfect romantic evening?

▶ **2.**

TIP: *Since the husbands are answering these same questions, you could add a twist for this* **Warm Up**: *Have someone in each group take notes on the answers given for questions one and two. Then exchange these notes and let each group see how the other answered the questions.*

3. How can the sexual dimension of marriage bring pressure to the relationship?

▶ **3.**

I. How Pressure Affects the Sexual Relationship

Case Study

(15-20 minutes)

Reid and Susan struggled to keep their passion in check during their courtship and engagement. They were both Christians and were committed to purity, and they experienced the fruits of that commitment after they were married. During their first three years they enjoyed a regular sexual relationship that was satisfying to both of them.

But things began to change after they had two children within two years. Here is a typical day for Reid and Susan now, during their seventh year of marriage:

6:00-7:15 A.M.: Wake up, eat, prepare for work, feed and dress the kids.

7:15-8:00 A.M.: Reid leaves for his 30-minute drive to his job at a bank; Susan drops off one child at day-care and another at preschool, then drives 15 minutes to the hospital where she works as a nurse.

6:00 P.M.: Susan arrives home exhausted after picking up kids and shopping for groceries; she starts getting dinner ready.

6:30 P.M.: Reid arrives home with a glazed look in his eyes.

6:30-7:00 P.M.: Dinner, clean kitchen.

7:00-8:30 P.M.: Take care of kids—games, baths, bedtime.

8:30-10:00 or 11:00 P.M.: Television, phone calls, catching up on unfinished work, paying bills, etc.

10:00 or 11:00 P.M.: Bedtime.

Reid and Susan feel that their life-style is too hectic, but they don't know how to change it. It seems they hardly ever get a chance to spend time together the way they used to. Once they finally get the kids to sleep and other responsibilities taken care of, all they feel like doing is watching television or sleeping.

Both Reid and Susan are frustrated with their sex life. Reid can't understand why Susan doesn't want to make love as much as she used to. Susan feels pressure to have sex more often than she wants. She resents Reid's sex drive and wonders how he can just jump into bed and start making love when they have hardly talked to each other for days.

On top of that, Susan has had trouble losing weight after bearing two children. She doesn't feel pretty, and she feels hurt when Reid makes remarks about "losing that flab." And Reid doesn't feel as attracted to Susan anymore. Other wives lose their post-baby weight and keep their good looks, so why can't Susan? At the same time, Reid isn't as trim as he used to be, either, though Susan hesitates to say anything about it.

The irony is that both Reid and Susan are still interested in sex. But they have drifted apart; the romance is gone. It seems the only time they can get together is during the weekend, and not always then.

A. What are the main pressures and problems that Reid and Susan are experiencing?

►**A.**

ANSWER: *They have an extremely busy schedule, with both partners working. When they have any time to focus on each other, they are usually exhausted. What time they do have is often spent watching television. They don't understand each other's needs in the sexual area. They are too concerned with outward appearance.*

B. How can misunderstanding your mate's needs create pressure in your marriage and in the sexual dimension of your relationship?

►**B.**

ANSWER: *It's easy to forget that your mate's needs are usually different from yours. It causes frustration when you expect your mate to feel or act the same way you do. For example, a woman may proceed more slowly while making love than her husband wants her to.*

C. How has a busy schedule, with its accompanying pressure and responsibility, affected your sexual relationship?

►**C.**

TIP: *Be prepared with a specific example from your own relationship. This will help the others think of similar instances.*

D. How does stress affect men and women in this area?

▶ **D.**

ANSWER: *In a general sense, stress can heighten the need for sexual release in a man. For the woman, it can heighten the need for a stronger relationship. Also, stress can easily cause conflict between a husband and wife, and when conflict occurs, the sexual relationship will suffer.*

II. THE PRIORITY OF THE SEXUAL RELATIONSHIP IN MARRIAGE

(5-10 minutes)

A. Read 1 Corinthians 7:5. What warning does this verse contain?

▶ **A.**

ANSWER: *A husband and wife need to "stop depriving one another" so that Satan has no foothold to tempt them.*

B. It seems this passage tells us to be deliberate about making the sexual relationship in marriage a priority. What are some practical ways you can do this?

▶ **B.**

TIP: *This question will be answered through the material in Part III of* **Blueprints**. *For now, see how your group members can answer the question. If they have trouble, ask, "Have you struggled with making it a priority in your marriage?"*

C. What are the primary activities that rob the two of you of time to spend together?

▶ **C.**
- ❑ Watching TV
- ❑ Reading
- ❑ Children
- ❑ Hobbies, sports or recreational activities
- ❑ Work
- ❑ Church activities
- ❑ Civic activities
- ❑ Other_____

TIP: *This is a crucial area in which to challenge your group. Many couples could spend more time cultivating their relationship if only they were committed to doing so. Television is an especially big robber of time. You might want to use this optional question: "What changes could you make in order to have more time to spend together?"*

*H*OMEBUILDERS *P*RINCIPLE

Couples need to make their sexual relationship a high priority.

11

III. How You Can Reduce Pressure in Your Sexual Relationship

(30-45 minutes)

A. Understand your husband's needs.

1. From your own experience, what is the most important lesson you have learned about how sex is different for a man and a woman?

▶ **1.**

▶ **2.** In his book, *His Needs, Her Needs,* Willard Harley lists the following needs in a marriage: admiration, affection, an attractive spouse, honesty and openness, family commitment, conversation, domestic support, recreational companionship, sexual fulfillment and financial support.

a. On the chart below, rank from 1 (most important) to 5 (least important) how you think *men* prioritized these needs. Then do the same thing for *women* on the right.

Men		Women
____	Admiration	____
____	Affection	____
____	An attractive spouse	____
____	Honesty and openness	____
____	Family commitment	____
____	Conversation	____
____	Domestic support	____
____	Recreational companionship	____
____	Sexual fulfillment	____
____	Financial support	____

TIP: *Have the women explain their rankings.*

b. Discuss the answers to the survey found in the group leader's guide. (Answers also can be found at the end of this session.)

ANSWER: *The top five needs for men were: 1. sexual fulfillment; 2. recreational companionship; 3. an attractive spouse; 4. domestic support; 5. admiration. The top five for women were: 1. affection; 2. conversation; 3. honesty and openness; 4. financial support; 5. family commitment.*

3. Read Ephesians 5:33b. What are some practical things you can do to give your husband respect as a man?

▶ 3.

4. Think for a moment about how your husband's need for respect relates to him sexually. How can a wife communicate respect and affirmation to a husband who has a stronger felt need for sex than she does?

▶ 4.

Another difference between men and women in this area is that, for a man, sex is more closely tied to his sense of self-worth. As Jill Renich points out in her book, *To Have and to Hold,* "Sex is the most meaningful demonstration of love and self-worth [for a man]. It is a part of his own deepest person." And contrary to popular images in the media, many men are "far more apprehensive when it comes to sex than a woman might believe," writes Dr. Joyce Brothers.

5. In what ways have you seen this in your marriage?

▶ **5.**

6. What advice would you give the woman who is more interested in love-making than her husband?

▶ **6.**

ANSWER: *First, understand the cause: A man's own feelings of insecurity or past rejection with his wife may affect his sex drive. Other inhibitors are pressure at work, past sexual abuse, and fear of failure. Also, for the last 20 years our culture has feminized men and sought to take away their initiative and leadership toward their wives. Second, discuss the problem as a couple and make adjustments in your schedule. If necessary talk to a qualified Christian counselor.*

B. Be more considerate of your mate's needs.

1. Read Philippians 2:3,4. Why do you think that an unselfish attitude is essential to a mutually fulfilling sex life with your husband?

▶ **1.** _____

ANSWER: *In these verses we are commanded to consider the needs of others as more important than our own. The sexual dimension of marriage works the best when both husband and wife are concerned with pleasing each other, meeting each other's needs.*

NOTE: *Humility means having a proper perspective of ourselves. It doesn't mean we should deny our needs or put ourselves down. Yet, the basis of our self-worth is our identity in Christ.*

TIP: *If you think your group is open enough, here's an optional question: "How has selfishness had a negative impact on your marriage?"*

2. What is one thing you've done to battle selfishness in this area?

▶ **2.** _____

HOMEBUILDERS PRINCIPLE

To build true sexual intimacy,
defeat selfishness by focusing
on what your mate needs.

12

C. Court your husband.

1. Think back to when you first dated your husband. What did you do to gain his attention and add romance to your relationship?

1.

2. Why do so many couples stop courting each other after they are married?

2.

ANSWER: Many lose their motivation after marriage, as if the "battle is won." In reality, of course, the "battle" never stops. You need to continue courting and seeking to please each other.

3. If appropriate, share one creative idea of how you or another person you know has managed to add romance to the marriage relationship. (You may want to write down any good ideas that other group members contribute!)

3.

Answer for Blueprints Question 2a. The top five needs for men were: 1. sexual fulfillment; 2. recreational companionship; 3. an attractive spouse; 4. domestic support; 5. admiration. The top five for women were: 1. affection; 2. conversation; 3. honesty and openness; 4. financial support; 5. family commitment.

Make a Date

*Ask everyone to look at the **Make a Date** section of the personal study guide and to take a moment to agree with their mate on a time this week to complete the **HomeBuilders Project**. Remind them that at the next session you will ask them to share one experience from this interaction.*

Set a date with your mate to meet in the next few days to complete **HomeBuilders Project #5**. Your leader will ask at the next session for you to share one thing from this experience.

Date	Time	Location

Recommended Reading

*Call attention to the **Recommended Reading**.*

Intended for Pleasure, by Ed and Gaye Wheat.

Here is a book that will bring you to a fuller awareness of the pleasures that can be found in God-directed sexual union. The Wheats apply what the Bible has to say about sex to our everyday lives in a meaningful way.

The Questions Book for Marriage Intimacy
by Dennis and Barbara Rainey.

This short book offers 31 questions you've probably never thought to ask your mate. These questions will ignite your curiosity and rekindle your fascination for each other. These questions will spark many memorable hours of sharing, sharpen your understanding of your mate and stimulate closeness in new areas of your marriage.

Dismiss in prayer, or invite group members to volunteer one-sentence prayers asking God's help in handling sexual pressures in their marriages.

Invite everyone to enjoy a time of refreshments and fellowship.

HomeBuilders Project #5

1. Complete the following exercise to judge how you and your mate handle the following aspects of your sexual relationship. Circle the number that corresponds to your answer. Draw an X through the number you think your mate will select.

	Low				High
The relationship we enjoy prior to lovemaking.	1	2	3	4	5
Viewing sex with positive anticipation.	1	2	3	4	5
The way you decide to have sex together.	1	2	3	4	5
The amount of communication during lovemaking (i.e. giving feedback, expressing desires, etc.).	1	2	3	4	5
Frequency of physical intimacy.	1	2	3	4	5
Gentleness and tenderness during lovemaking.	1	2	3	4	5
Variety of sexual experiences together.	1	2	3	4	5
Understanding of one another in this area.	1	2	3	4	5

2. Do you fully trust your mate with your body? If not, in what aspect do you feel distrust? Why? Refer to 1 Corinthians 7:3-5.

3. List any incorrect attitudes you may have about your body or your mate's body. Refer to Song of Solomon 5:1-16; 7:1-9.

4. Complete the following to share later with your mate:

a. When we are sharing physical love, I like for you to . . .

b. It makes me feel discouraged when you . . .

5. What are two things you can do to decrease the pressure either or both of you may feel in your sexual relationship?

6. Look back over the points we covered during the session on sexual intimacy. What are the top three things you think would really please your mate?

7. Evaluate before God whether there is any bitterness in your heart toward your mate regarding your sexual relationship . Read 1 John 1:9 and confess any anger or resentment that may have built up toward your mate.

INTERACT AS A COUPLE: 30 MINUTES

1. Share with each other what you wrote during the individual time.

2. Choose three decisions you can make together that will improve your sexual relationship.

3. Schedule a whole day and night within the next month when the two of you can get away for a special time of communication and intimacy.

4. Pray together and thank God for each other as His provision for each other's sexual needs. Make a commitment to each other to improve communication and intimacy.

Remember to bring your calendar to the next
session you can **Make a Date.**

DRAWING MORAL BOUNDARIES

(ETHICAL PRESSURES)

OBJECTIVES

In this session you will lead your group members to:

- Discuss how today's moral ambiguity affects them and their marriages;
- Look at some Scriptures which show that this problem is not a new one; and
- Consider some ways to establish moral boundaries.

OVERALL COMMENTS

1. As our culture slides further and further from a biblical standard of morality, Christians are influenced by the world in ways they might not even realize. Often we are so influenced by the world that we fail to recognize areas in which we need to draw moral boundaries. This session will help your group members confront some of these areas and give them a framework in which to draw boundaries.

2. One reason some issues are difficult to work through is that the Bible does not directly

address them. For example, there was no television, and no movies, in biblical times. Yet the Scriptures do provide guidelines that we can apply. In the process of applying God's Word and drawing moral boundaries, however, we need to recognize that one person's boundaries may differ from another.

This does not mean that we agree with the worldly mind-set that "my morality is as good as yours." That mind-set leaves God and His Word completely out of the equation. The important thing to emphasize to your group members is that they seek to form boundaries in their lives which glorify God and harmonize with His Word. Doing this provides a solid foundation for our moral decisions.

3. Since this is the final session, be sure to leave enough time for the conclusion, in which you'll ask questions about the entire study. This is a good time for you to reiterate the major theme of the study: how our decisions affect the degree of pressure we feel in our family life. It's also a good time for couples to recall what they've learned from the study—and from each other. Finally, use the opportunity to challenge your couples to continue applying what they've learned.

Today's marriages are being undermined by a spreading amoral fog that blankets our world. Defining together our living standards—on both a biblical and a practical basis—is a key ingredient for building a strong, secure marriage.

(10-15 minutes)

1. If a missionary couple returned to America today after serving in a primitive part of Africa for 20 years, what moral changes would they notice in our country?

▶ **1.**

ANSWER: *Immorality has always been evident in our society, but someone who has been gone for 20 years would notice many changes. Among other things, they would notice that we've become a more violent and sex-saturated society. They would notice that many things that were generally considered wrong or immoral 20 years ago are being accepted or condoned today. If they looked closely, they would find that Christians who stand up for biblical morality are increasingly being portrayed in the secular media as fanatics and bigots.*

2. What moral changes would they notice among today's Christians?

▶**2.**

ANSWER: *They would likely notice that many Christians continue to drift along with the world. As always, Christians may speak up against wrong, but their lives may not reflect what they say is true.*

3. What would you tell them were the causes behind these changes?

▶**3.**

ANSWER: *We are not willing today to draw moral lines or define our lines morally. We leave too many things open—we are too tolerant of evil, and it has gained much ground in our lives. Also, we are more suspicious of authority figures, and less willing to accept what we're taught before thinking it through.*

I. Our Slide into Moral Ambiguity

(10-15 minutes)

James Hunter writes in his book, *Evangelicalism*, that words such as "worldly" and "worldliness" have, within a generation, "lost most of their traditional meanings....The moral boundaries separating Christian conduct from worldly conduct has been substantially undermined."

Many marriages suffer from moral ambiguity. Our world has increasingly defined "right and wrong" as "what is right and wrong for *you*." Moral absolutes that once defined the quality and character of one's life are now being replaced with a chameleon kind of value system that has no more depth than a passing fad. A marriage built on a shifting, morally superficial foundation is clearly in trouble from the start.

TIP: *Have someone in your group read the above statement.*

What are some ways that you, as a Christian, feel the pressure to change your views on specific moral issues?

TIP: *If discussion is slow, mention a couple of possibilities: "How are we pressured to change our views on premarital sex?" "How are we pressured to change our views on homosexuality?"*

The good news is that a couple willing to take their biblical beliefs and translate them into strong, practical statements of moral conviction will escape a host of unnecessary hurts and pressures. The result will be freedom, not confusion; stability and unity rather than conflict and suffering.

II. MORALITY THEN AND NOW

(10-15 minutes)

A. Look at the concluding statement of the book of Judges (21:25). How is one of the bleakest moral periods in Israel's history summed up?

▶ **A.**

ANSWER: *"Every one did what was right in his own eyes." No standards!*

B. What specifics does Hosea use to describe the moral conditions of his day (Hosea 4:1-6)?

▶ **B.**

ANSWER: *The sins of faithlessness, swearing, deception, murder, stealing, adultery, bloodshed, and violence. Verse 4 talks of no one's finding fault with this or offering reproof. Hosea describes a society in which everything is relative. It's a "do your own thing" world with—again—no standards.*

TIP: *Have someone who doesn't talk much answer this one.*

C. What insight does Hosea offer as to the cause behind this moral decay? (See v. 6.)

▶C.

ANSWER: *There is no knowledge of God; they have forgotten His law.*

D. How are these statements relevant to what we are seeing in our present-day society?

▶D.

ANSWER: *We see the same conditions in our society today. Because people are drifting away from God and fewer people are acknowledging His law as relevant to today's society, our culture is crumbling.*

TIP: *If your group members are answering too generally, ask them questions about specific ways that they see morality changing at their job, with their friends, etc.*

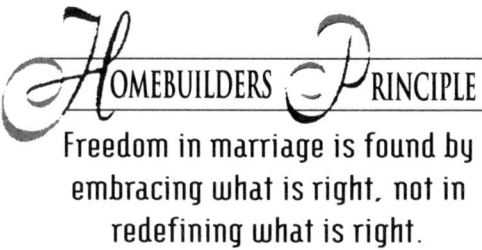

HOMEBUILDERS PRINCIPLE

Freedom in marriage is found by embracing what is right, not in redefining what is right.

13

III. MORALITY AND YOUR MARRIAGE

(10-15 minutes)

A. In what specific areas do couples need to establish practical moral standards for their homes? As a group, make a collective list.

A.

ANSWER: *Money, television, time with children, work schedule, etc.*

B. What can make it hard for couples to establish these standards? Take your time and think deeply here.

B.

ANSWER: *Sometimes it's a lack of discipline, of finding the time and commitment to decide what is right or wrong and enforce these standards. Also, a couple may not have really thought through what they believe and how to apply biblical teachings to different areas of their lives. Or it may just be that they want to go on doing what they want no matter what God says. Or they may not be aware of how much impact a lack of definition will have on their marriage and children.*

C. A marriage is always in motion, either toward health or sickness, toward oneness or isolation. How can the health of a marriage be undermined by a couple's unwillingness to draw clear, practical boundaries of moral conviction for themselves?

C.

ANSWER: *We are continually pressured to believe that discarding our "outdated morality" will free us up to realize our true potential as human beings. In reality, the moral ambiguity of today's society can tempt us to engage in behaviors that are destructive to ourselves and to the relationships most impor-*

tant to us. For example, if you begin to believe that adultery would not be that bad, you may make a choice that would inflict a painful or even fatal wound on your marriage relationship and on the person God has placed in your life to be your mate.

D. In what areas have you felt the immoral undertow of our world pulling at your life and marriage?

▶ **D.** _____

_____

_____

TIP: *This is an important question, because it asks couples to be vulnerable about struggles they face. If they need prompting, ask a question like, "Is it hard for you to decide what movies to watch?"*

E. What have you done as an individual to resist this pressure?

▶ **E.** _____

_____

_____

F. What have you done as a couple?

▶ **F.** _____

_____

_____

IV. Some Considerations for Drawing Moral Boundaries

(10-15 minutes)

The Word of God is always the starting point in moral considerations. In some areas the Scriptures draw clear and specific moral lines. Sexual immorality, for instance, is addressed in black-and-white terms and should not be a moral issue in dispute.

But there are other issues within everyday life where a couple will not find so succinct a biblical statement—issues such as the use of money, debt, work and what it takes from a marriage, the use of alcohol, the types of movies and television programming we allow ourselves to view, time with one another and with children, etc. These, too, are moral issues with serious ramifications for any marriage. And without sound biblical thinking and workable application in these areas and many more, the pressure of worldly conformity soon replaces "the peaceful fruit of righteousness" (Hebrews 12:11). We need to take the time and effort to think through these issues and develop our standards. Unexamined acceptance of someone else's standards sets us up for weak moral boundaries that fail under pressure.

Let's explore some biblical guidelines for drawing boundaries and convictions in these "not-so-clear" areas.

A. Read Titus 2:11-14. What are we exhorted to do in verses 11 and 12?

▶ **A.**

ANSWER: *The first exhortation is to deny ungodliness and worldly desires. The second exhortation is to live sensibly, righteously and godly. This second exhortation is key to the questions that follow.*

B. Moral conviction in a marriage will follow the pattern outlined by the three word pictures in verse 12. Any moral boundary a couple draws for themselves should do three things:

It should make good, practical sense (a definition of "sensibly").

It should be fair and just to all (a definition of "righteously").

It should meet with God's approval and harmonize with His Word (a definition of "godly").

NOTE: Some couples have had standards forced upon them by others. Then, seeking to escape this pressure, they've basically decided to avoid altogether questions about moral standards. This session is not intended to force standards upon you from the outside, but to encourage you to select a definitive moral standard for yourself that harmonizes with the biblical guidelines above.

Also, one of the chief arguments against establishing clear moral standards is the cry of "legalism." The goal of this session is to help you establish personal standards which you can justify and defend before the liberating Word of God. In doing so, you will find the freedom God's Word promises.

C. Now let's apply those three guidelines. Pick one of the situations in the next column and determine how these guidelines (living sensibly, righteously and godly) help in evaluating the morality of the situation:

▶ **C.**

The husband or wife who works consistently 60-70 hours per week.

The use of alcohol by one marriage partner when the other is offended.

Watching television shows that include numerous illicit sexual situations and instances of offensive language.

TIP: *With each situation, make sure the group discusses all three guidelines as listed above. For example, ask, "How could the standard of living 'sensibly' apply here?" Be prepared for some disagreements in the discussion.*

D. According to Romans 14:19,21,22, what else needs to be considered in the moral guidelines we draw?

▶ **D.**

ANSWER: *How our actions affect other people, especially new, impressionable or "weaker" Christians.*

E. Who ultimately is affected by our moral clarity (or lack of it) in everyday life...

▶ **E.**

...as stated negatively in Romans 2:23,24?

ANSWER: *When we fail to hold to clear moral standards, we dishonor God and allow nonbelievers to ridicule and blaspheme Him.*

...as stated positively in Matthew 5:16?

▶

ANSWER: *When we do hold to clear moral standards, we let the world see our good works and glorify our Father in heaven.*

...as stated in terms of the legacy we leave in Exodus 20:5?

▶

ANSWER: *Our moral failings will be visited on our children and on subsequent generations.*

HOMEBUILDERS PRINCIPLE

If your Christianity is not
defined practically, it will be
practically worthless.

14

Construction

(to be completed as a couple)
(5-10 minutes)
Let's take a look at just one area where we need
to establish boundaries.

1. What practical moral lines have you drawn together (until now) about the *movies you watch*? The secular world has drawn its guidelines—G, PG, PG13, R, NC-17. But how do you decide what movies you will watch? List your practical standards. Honesty is very important here!

▶ **1.** _____

_____

_____

_____

_____

_____

_____

_____

_____

_____

_____

2. How did you arrive at these boundaries? What biblical guidelines did you use (if any) in establishing your standards? Do you both feel good about the standards you hold in this area?

▶ **2.**

3. What pressures are associated with indecision in this area or with one person making the decisions? Who could get hurt?

▶ **3.**

4. If you don't agree on these guidelines, what steps can you take to find a common moral ground you both can be accountable to uphold?

▶ **4.**

V. THE FINAL CONCLUSION

(10-15 minutes)

A. As you look back over this entire study on *Managing Pressure in Your Marriage*, what have been the highlights for you?

▶ **A.**

B. What are the most important things you've learned?

▶ **B.**

C. What is the most important application point which you need to implement?

▶ **C.**

HOMEBUILDERS PRINCIPLE

A couple cannot face the pressures of today's amoral culture unless they walk together in agreement with their standards.

15

Ask everyone to look at the Make a Date section of the personal study guide and to take a moment to agree with their mate on a time this week to complete the HomeBuilders Project.

Set a date with your mate to meet in the next few days to complete **HomeBuilders Project #6.**

Date	**Time**	**Location**

Recommended Reading

*Call attention to the **Recommended Reading**.*

Against the Night, by Charles Colson.

In this book Chuck Colson challenges Christians to regain a vision of what it means to live as members of the Kingdom of God and to be the people of God. Page by page, he maps out a strategy for all who are determined to stand faithfully in the midst of the present darkness. In so doing, he rekindles our spiritual passion for goodness, for justice, for righteousness, and for living as lights amid the gathering darkness.

Why Johnny Can't Tell Right from Wrong
by William Kilpatrick.

In what may be the most important and most controversial book about public education in America in decades, William Kilpatrick argues that our schools are failing to provide the moral education they once did. The best way to encourage moral growth, says Kilpatrick, is to return to the proven model of character education, with its emphasis on good example and good habits of behavior. Kilpatrick explains why this approach works, and he gives examples of school systems that have switched to character education with impressive results.

Dismiss in prayer, or invite group members to volunteer one-sentence prayers asking God's help in handling the pressure of weariness in their marriages.

Invite everyone to enjoy a time of refreshments and fellowship.

HomeBuilders Project #6

INDIVIDUALLY: 30 MINUTES

1. What pressure points do you feel in your marriage that may be the result of moral indecisiveness? List below.

_____

_____

_____

_____

2. How do you feel about the guidelines you have drawn in the following areas? (Add to the list anything else you feel is important). Rate your feelings using a scale of 1-5, with 1 being "uncertain, uneasy and disturbed" and 5 being "clear, confident and secure."

____ Environment (of earth)	____ Business expense reports
____ Pornography	____ Types of entertainment
____ Use of alcohol	____ Dress
____ Paying taxes	____ Sexual freedom
____ TV/cable	____ Adultery
____ Movies	____ Eating
____ Gambling	____ Exaggerating
____ Abortion	____ Lying
____ Debt	____ Drugs
____ Divorce	____ My role in our marriage

____ Profanity
____ Church giving
____ Types of friends
____ Ministry involvement and our marriage

____ My mate's role in our marriage
____ Church attendance
____ Abusive language to mate
____ Others:_____

3. In some marriages, one person does not respect the other's individual moral boundaries, and tries to nag and pressure the mate to do things that are offensive to them. Is this true in your marriage? If so...

Is there something you can cease doing so that you would honor your mate?

Is there something you can release your mate to do without making your mate feel guilty?

INTERACT AS A COUPLE: 30-60 MINUTES

PART ONE:

1. Begin by reading Ephesians 4:29-32 together.

2. Look back at the list you each completed under question 2 of the individual section. Share your conclusions with your mate. What are some standards you feel you need to begin establishing as a couple in different areas?

3. At what points are there wide differences in opinion between the two of you? Discuss those differences together, seeking resolution and oneness. Remember: Two must be agreed if they are to walk together well.

4. Share your thoughts on question 3 in the individual section if it applies. Seek to resolve whatever conflicts may be there, remembering to "give preference to one another in honor" (Romans 12:10).

PART TWO:

1. How has your participation in this HomeBuilders study helped your marriage?

2. What are the most important decisions you've made?

3. What are the most important decisions you still need to make?

4. Close in prayer, thanking God for the time you've spent together as a couple.

Conclusion

WHERE DO YOU GO FROM HERE?

Congratulations! You are a member of a rapidly expanding, worldwide movement of couples who desire to be HomeBuilders. By completing this study you have made an investment in your marriage and family that will pay off for generations. But this study is not the end, it's merely a part of a process that you need to continue for your good and for the sake of your friends' marriages and families.

So we have a challenge for you:

If you've led this HomeBuilders study, then we encourage you to select two or three other couples from your group to "spin off" another group and lead a HomeBuilders study of their own in their neighborhood. If you've been a group member then you ought to consider leading one of these studies—that is how you will really learn the material! There are several studies to choose from: *Building Your Marriage, Building Your Mate's Self-Esteem, Building Teamwork in Your Marriage, Mastering Money in Your Marriage, Resolving Conflict in Your Marriage, Growing Together in Christ,* and *Life Choices for a Lasting Marriage.*

And, if you need help in selecting which study is best for your group, call our helpful Customer Service Representative at 1-800-333-1433 and just ask—we will be delighted to be a resource for you. Additional ministries and outreaches of FamilyLife include:

1. "FamilyLife Today": This daily, 25-minute program can be heard on top Christian radio stations across the country. Your host on the program is Executive Director of FamilyLife, Dennis Rainey.

"FamilyLife Today" presents a format that is conversational in nature and provides you with biblical insights and practical how-to's for successful marriage and family relationships.

2. FamilyLife Marriage Conference: This conference offers powerful messages that will help you learn about God's plan for marriage, and by completing our practical couples projects, you and your mate could experience the positive difference God's principles can make.

3. FamilyLife Parenting Conference: This conference will help you clarify your convictions and assist you, as a parent, in evaluating your relationships with your children. You'll also have the opportunity to take practical steps to help your children mature in their emotional, sexual and spiritual identities.

4. Urban Family Conference: We take the content from the FamilyLife Marriage Conference and tailor it to different audiences, schedules, and cultures. We are working in conjunction with Campus Crusade for Christ's Legacy ministry to host these conferences nationwide.

Call for information and free brochures on any of our weekend conferences.

Will you join us in "Touching Lives And Changing Families"?

The following are some practical ways you can make a difference in families today:

1. If you are not a part of a growing church, join one. (If you haven't been baptized as a believer in Jesus Christ, take that step, too.)

2. Gather a group of couples (four to seven) and lead them through the six sessions of the HomeBuilders study you just completed.

3. Commit to participate in another study from The HomeBuilders Couples Series™.

4. Begin weekly family nights—teaching your children about Christ, the Bible, and the Christian life.

5. Show the film, *JESUS*, on video as an evangelistic outreach in your neighborhood. For more information, write to:
Inspirational Media
30012 Ivy Glenn Dr., Suite 200
Laguna Niguel, CA 92677

6. Host an evangelistic dinner party. Invite your non-Christian friends to your home and as a couple share your faith in Christ and the forgiveness of His gospel.

7. Share the good news of Jesus Christ with neighborhood children.

8. If you have attended the FamilyLife Marriage Conference, why not use the material you received to assist your pastor in premarital counseling?

For more information on any of the above ministry opportunities, contact your local church or write:
FamilyLife
P.O. Box 23840
Little Rock, AR 72221-3840
(501) 223-8663

About the Author:

Dennis Rainey, co-author of this study and Senior Editor of The HomeBuilders Couples Series™, is Executive Director of FamilyLife, a ministry of Campus Crusade for Christ. He is featured daily on the "FamilyLife Today" radio program on stations across the country. Dennis and his wife, Barbara, have six children and live near Little Rock, Arkansas.

Robert Lewis has been a teaching pastor at Fellowship Bible Church in Little Rock, Arkansas since 1980. He has spoken nationally and internationally with FamilyLife of Campus Crusade for Christ for over 5 years. He also coauthored the book, *Rocking the Roles*. Robert and his wife, Sherard, have been married for 17 years and have four children.

THE FOUR SPIRITUAL LAWS*

Just as there are physical laws that govern the physical universe, so are there spiritual laws that govern your relationship with God.

> **LAW ONE: God loves you and offers a wonderful plan for your life.**

God's Love

"For God so loved the world, that He gave His only begotten Son, that whoever believes in Him should not perish, but have eternal life" (John 3:16).

God's Plan

(Christ speaking) "I came that they might have life, and might have it abundantly" (that it might be full and meaningful) (John 10:10).

Why is it that most people are not experiencing the abundant life? Because...

> **LAW TWO: Man is sinful and separated from God. Therefore, he cannot know and experience God's love and plan for his life.**

*Written by Bill Bright. Copyright © Campus Crusade for Christ, Inc., 1965, all rights reserved.

Man Is Sinful

"For all have sinned and fall short of the glory of God" (Romans 3:23).

Man was created to have fellowship with God; but, because of his stubborn self-will, chose to go his own independent way, and fellowship with God was broken. This self-will, characterized by an attitude of active rebellion or passive indifference, is evidence of what the Bible calls sin.

Man Is Separated

"For the wages of sin is death" (spiritual separation from God) (Romans 6:23).

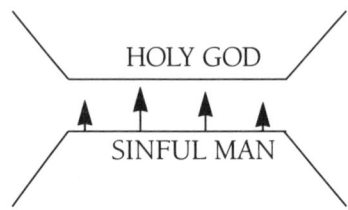

This diagram illustrates that God is holy and man is sinful. A great gulf separates the two. The arrows illustrate that man is continually trying to reach God and the abundant life through his own efforts, such as a good life, philosophy, or religion.

The third law explains the only way to bridge this gulf...

LAW THREE: Jesus Christ is God's only provision for man's sin. Through Him you can know and experience God's love and plan for your life.

He Died in Our Place

"But God demonstrates His own love toward us, in that while we were yet sinners, Christ died for us" (Romans 5:8).

He Rose from the Dead

"Christ died for our sins . . . He was buried . . . He was raised on the third day according to the Scriptures . . . He appeared to [Peter], then to the twelve. After that He appeared to more than five hundred . . ." (1 Corinthians 15:3-6).

He Is the Only Way to God

"Jesus said to him, 'I am the way, and the truth, and the life; no one comes to the Father, but through Me'" (John 14:6).

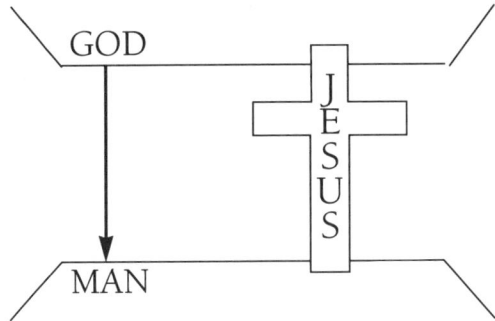

  This diagram illustrates that God has bridged the gulf that separates us from Him by sending His Son, Jesus Christ, to die on the cross in our place to pay the penalty for our sins.

  It is not enough just to know these three laws . . .

> **LAW FOUR: We must individually receive Jesus Christ as Savior and Lord; then we can know and experience God's love and plan for our lives.**

We Must Receive Christ

"But as many as received Him, to them He gave the right to become children of God, even to those who believe in His name" (John 1:12).

We Receive Christ Through Faith

"For by grace you have been saved through faith; and that not of your-selves, it is the gift of God; not as a result of works, that no one should boast" (Ephesians 2:8,9).

When We Receive Christ, We Experience a New Birth

(Read John 3:1-8.)

We Receive Christ by Personal Invitation

(Christ is speaking) "Behold, I stand at the door and knock; if any one hears My voice and opens the door, I will come in to him" (Revelation 3:20).

Receiving Christ involves turning to God from self (repentance) and trusting Christ to come into our lives to forgive our sins and to make us the kind of people He wants us to be. Just to agree intellectually that Jesus Christ is the Son of God and that He died on the cross for our sins is not enough. Nor is it enough to have an emotional experience. We receive Jesus Christ by faith, as an act of the will.

These two circles represent two kinds of lives:

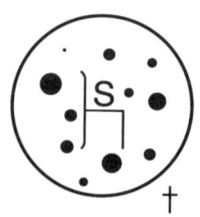

SELF-DIRECTED LIFE

S — Self is on the throne
† — Christ is outside the life
• — Interests are directed by self, often resulting in discord and frustration

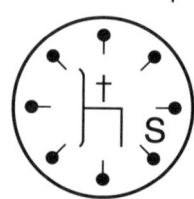

CHRIST-DIRECTED LIFE

† — Christ is in the life and on the throne
S — Self is yielding to Christ
• — Interests are directed by Christ, resulting in harmony with God's plan

Which circle best represents your life?
Which circle would you like to have represent your life?
The following explains how you can receive Christ:

You Can Receive Christ Right Now by Faith Through Prayer

(Prayer is talking with God.)
God knows your heart and is not so concerned with your words as He is with the attitude of your heart. The following is a suggested prayer:

> Lord Jesus, I need You. Thank You for dying on the cross for my sins. I open the door of my life and receive You as my Savior and Lord. Thank You for forgiving my sins and giving me eternal life. Make me the kind of person You want me to be.

Does this prayer express the desire of your heart?
If it does, pray this prayer right now, and Christ will come into your life, as He promised.

HAVE YOU MADE THE WONDERFUL DISCOVERY OF THE SPIRIT-FILLED LIFE?*

Every day can be an exciting adventure for the Christian who knows the reality of being filled with the Holy Spirit and who lives constantly, moment by moment, under His gracious control.

The Bible tells us that there are three kinds of people:

1. NATURAL MAN (one who has not received Christ)

"But a natural man does not accept the things of the Spirit of God; for they are foolishness to him, and he cannot understand them, because they are spiritually appraised" (1 Corinthians 2:14).

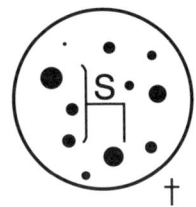

SELF-DIRECTED LIFE
S— Ego or finite self is on the throne
† — Christ is outside the life
• — Interests are controlled by self, often resulting in discord and frustration

2. SPIRITUAL MAN (one who is controlled and empowered by the Holy Spirit)

"But he who is spiritual appraises all things..." (1 Corinthians 2:15).

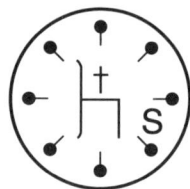

CHRIST-DIRECTED LIFE
† — Christ on the throne of the life
S — Ego or self is dethroned
• — Interests are under control of infinite God, resulting in harmony with God's plan

3. CARNAL MAN (one who has received Christ, but who lives in defeat because he trusts in his own efforts to live the Christian life)

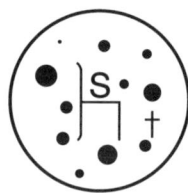

SELF-DIRECTED LIFE
S — Ego or finite self is on the throne
† — Christ is dethroned
• — Interests controlled by self, often resulting in discord and frustration

"And I, brethren, could not speak to you as to spiritual men, but as to carnal men, as to babes in Christ. I gave you milk to drink, not solid food; for you were not yet able to receive it. Indeed, even now you are not yet able, for you are still carnal. For since there is jealousy and strife among you, are you not fleshly, and are you not walking like mere men?" (1 Corinthians 3:1-3).

A. God Has Provided for Us an Abundant and Fruitful Christian Life

Jesus said, "I came that they might have life, and might have it abundantly" (John 10:10).

"I am the vine, you are the branches; he who abides in Me, and I in him, he bears much fruit; for apart from Me you can do nothing" (John 15:5).

"But the fruit of the Spirit is love, joy, peace, patience, kindness, goodness, faithfulness, gentleness, self-control; against such things there is no law" (Galatians 5:22,23).

"But you shall receive power when the Holy Spirit has come upon you; and you shall be My witnesses both in Jerusalem, and in all Judea and Samaria, and even to the remotest part of the earth" (Acts 1:8).

THE SPIRITUAL MAN
Some Personal Traits that Result from Trusting God:

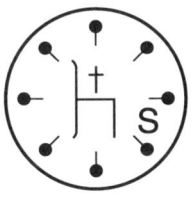

Christ-centered	Love
Empowered by the Holy Spirit	Joy
Introduces others to Christ	Peace
Effective prayer life	Patience
Understands God's Word	Kindness
Trusts God	Goodness
Obeys God	Faithfulness

The degree to which these traits are manifested in the life depends upon the extent to which the Christian trusts the Lord with every detail of his life, and upon his maturity in Christ. One who is only beginning to understand the ministry of the Holy Spirit should not be discouraged if he is not as fruitful as more mature Christians who have known and experienced this truth for a longer period.

Why is it that most Christians are not experiencing the abundant life?

B. CARNAL CHRISTIANS CANNOT EXPERIENCE THE ABUNDANT AND FRUITFUL CHRISTIAN LIFE

The carnal man trusts in his own efforts to live the Christian life:

1. He is either uninformed about, or has forgotten, God's love, forgiveness and power (Romans 5:8-10; Hebrews 10:1-25; 1 John 1; 2:1-3; 2 Peter 1:9; Acts 1:8).

2. He has an up-and-down spiritual experience.

3. He cannot understand himself—he wants to do what is right, but cannot.

4. He fails to draw upon the power of the Holy Spirit to live the Christian life.

(1 Corinthians 3:1-3; Romans 7:15-24; 8:7; Galatians 5:16-18)

THE CARNAL MAN

Some or all of the following traits may characterize the Christian who does not fully trust God:

Ignorance of his
   spiritual heritage
Unbelief
Disobedience
Loss of love for God
   and for others
Poor prayer life
No desire for Bible study

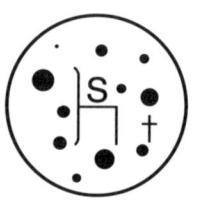

Legalistic attitude
Discouragement
Impure thoughts
Jealousy
Guilt
Critical spirit
Worry
Frustration
Aimlessness

(The individual who professes to be a Christian but who continues to practice sin should realize that he may not be a Christian at all, according to 1 John 2:3; 3:6,9; Ephesians 5:5.)

The third truth gives us the only solution to this problem...

C. JESUS PROMISED THE ABUNDANT AND FRUITFUL LIFE AS THE RESULT OF BEING FILLED (CONTROLLED AND EMPOWERED) BY THE HOLY SPIRIT

The Spirit-filled life is the Christ-controlled life by which Christ lives His life in and through us in the power of the Holy Spirit (John 15).

1. One becomes a Christian through the ministry of the Holy Spirit, according to John 3:1-8. From the moment of spiritual birth, the Christian is indwelt by the Holy Spirit at all times (John 1:12; Colossians 2:9,10; John 14:16,17). Though all Christians are indwelt by the Holy Spirit, not all Christians are filled (controlled and empowered) by the Holy Spirit.

2. The Holy Spirit is the source of the overflowing life (John 7:37-39).

3. The Holy Spirit came to glorify Christ (John 16:1-5). When one is filled with the Holy Spirit, he is a true disciple of Christ.

4. In His last command before His ascension, Christ promised the power of the Holy Spirit to enable us to be witnesses for Him (Acts 1:1-9).

How, then, can one be filled with the Holy Spirit?

D. WE ARE FILLED (CONTROLLED AND EMPOWERED) BY THE HOLY SPIRIT BY FAITH; THEN WE CAN EXPERIENCE THE ABUNDANT AND FRUITFUL LIFE THAT CHRIST PROMISED TO EACH CHRISTIAN

You can appropriate the filling of the Holy Spirit *right now* if you:

1. Sincerely desire to be controlled and empowered by the Holy Spirit (Matthew 5:6; John 7:37-39).

2. Confess your sins.

By faith thank God that He has forgiven all of your sins—past, present, and future—because Christ died for you (Colossians 2:13-15; 1 John 1; 2:1-3; Hebrews 10:1-17).

3. By faith claim the fullness of the Holy Spirit, according to:

a. HIS COMMAND—Be filled with the Spirit. "And do not get drunk with wine, for that is dissipation, but be filled with the Spirit" (Ephesians 5:18).

b. HIS PROMISE—He will always answer when we pray according to His will. "And this is the confidence which we have before Him, that, if we ask anything according to His will, He hears us. And if we know that He hears us in whatever we ask, we know that we have the requests which we have asked from Him" (1 John 5:14,15).

Faith can be expressed through prayer...

How to Pray in Faith to Be Filled with the Holy Spirit

We are filled with the Holy Spirit by faith alone. However, true prayer is one way of expressing your faith. The following is a suggested prayer:

Dear Father, I need You. I acknowledge that I have been in control of my life; and that, as a result, I have sinned against You. I thank You that You have forgiven my sins through Christ's death on the cross for me. I now invite Christ to again take control of the throne of my life. Fill me with the Holy Spirit as You commanded me to be filled, and as You promised in your Word that You would do if I asked in faith. I pray this in the name of Jesus. As an expression of my faith, I now thank You for taking control of my life and for filling me with the Holy Spirit.

Does this prayer express the desire of your heart? If so, bow in prayer and trust God to fill you with the Holy Spirit right now.

How to Know that You are Filled (Controlled and Empowered) by the Holy Spirit

Did you ask God to fill you with the Holy Spirit? Do you know that you are now filled with the Holy Spirit? On what authority? (On the trustworthiness of God Himself and His Word: Hebrews 11:6; Romans 14:22,23.)

Do not depend upon feelings. The promise of God's Word, not our feelings, is our authority. The Christian lives by faith (trust) in the trustworthiness of God Himself and His Word. This train diagram illustrates the relationship between fact (God and His Word), faith (our trust in God and His Word), and feeling (the result of our faith and obedience) (John 14:21).

The train will run with or without the caboose. However, it would be futile to attempt to pull the train by the caboose. In the same way, we, as Christians, do not depend upon feelings or emotions, but we place our faith (trust) in the trustworthiness of God and the promises of His Word.

How to Walk in the Spirit

Faith (trust in God and His promises) is the only means by which a Christian can live the Spirit-controlled life. As you continue to trust Christ moment by moment:

1. Your life will demonstrate more and more of the fruit of the Spirit (Galatians 5:22,23); and will be more and more conformed to the image of Christ (Romans 12:2; 2 Corinthians 3:18).

2. Your prayer life and study of God's Word will become more meaningful.

3. You will experience His power in witnessing (Acts 1:8).

4. You will be prepared for spiritual conflict against the world (1 John 2:15-17); against the flesh (Galatians 5:16,17); and against Satan (1 Peter 5:7-9; Ephesians 6:10-13).

5. You will experience His power to resist temptation and sin (1 Corinthians 10:13; Philippians 4:13; Ephesians 1:19-23; 6:10; 2 Timothy 1:7; Romans 6;1-16).

Spiritual Breathing

By faith you can continue to experience God's love and forgiveness.

If you become aware of an area of your life (an attitude or an action) that is displeasing to the Lord, even though you are walking with Him and sincerely desiring to serve Him, simply thank God that He has forgiven your sins—past, present and future—on the basis of Christ's death on the cross. Claim His love and forgiveness by faith and continue to have fellowship with Him.

If you retake the throne of your life through sin—a definite act of disobedience—breathe spiritually.

Spiritual Breathing (exhaling the impure and inhaling the pure) is an exercise in faith that enables you to continue to experience God's love and forgiveness.

1. Exhale—confess your sin—agree with God concerning your sin and thank Him for His forgiveness of it, according to 1 John 1:9 and Hebrews 10:1-25. Confession involves repentance—a change in attitude and action.

2. Inhale—surrender the control of your life to Christ, and appropriate (receive) the fullness of the Holy Spirit by faith. Trust that He now controls and empowers you, according to the command of Ephesians 5:18, and the promise of 1 John 5:14,15.

Renew Your Commitment.

Y ou've just finished an inspiring study from **The HomeBuilders Couples Series™.** No doubt you've learned a lot of things about your mate that will help the two of you grow closer together for years to come. You've also learned a lot about God's Word, and how much

it means to study the Bible with other couples. But don't let it stop here—lay the next block in the foundation of your marriage by beginning another **HomeBuilders** couples study. It will help you keep your marriage as strong, as dynamic, as solid as the day you said "I do."

Your Mate Is a Gift from God.

Growing together as one begins by accepting your husband or wife as God's perfect provision for your needs—and trusting that He knows what your needs are even better than you do. Receive your mate with open arms, and you'll begin to draw closer together—in incredible, heartfelt new ways.

Building Your Marriage
By Dennis Rainey
Study Guide S411172
Leader's Guide AB026

Turn Conflict into Love and Understanding.

Every marriage has its share of conflict. But you can turn conflict into something positive. Once you get into the habit of being a blessing even when you've been insulted, you'll discover for yourself that the result—a stronger, more exciting marriage—is well worth the effort.

Resolving Conflict in Your Marriage
By Bob & Jan Horner
Study Guide S411202
Leader's Guide AB031

Celebrate and Enjoy Your Differences.

Once you understand that your differences are gifts from God, you'll see how they can help you enjoy each other more and make your relationship fun, healthy and fascinating. You are the unique person who is equipped to complete and fulfill your mate!

Building Teamwork in Your Marriage
By Robert Lewis
Study Guide S411181
Leader's Guide AB028

Marriage Is God's Workshop for Self-Esteem.

When you both know you are accepted, appreciated and free to risk failure, you'll experience new levels of love and fulfillment—personally and as a couple. It starts by putting past hurts behind you and bringing positive words to your mate that will strengthen, heal and encourage. This study will show you how.

Building Your Mate's Self-Esteem
By Dennis & Barbara Rainey
Study Guide S411199
Leader's Guide AB030

FAMILYLIFE

Look for these **HomeBuilders** couples studies at your local Christian bookstore.
Coming in June 1993: *Mastering Money in Your Marriage* and *Growing Together in Christ.*
Coming in Oct. 1993: *Managing Pressure in Your Marriage* and *Life Choices for a Lasting Marriage.*

Gospel Light

"A Weekend to Remember"

Every couple has a unique set of needs. The FamilyLife Marriage Conference meets couples' needs by equipping them with proven solutions that address practically every component of "How to Build a Better Marriage." The conference gives you the opportunity to slow down and focus on your spouse and your relationship. You will spend an insightful weekend together, doing fun couples' projects and hearing from dynamic speakers on real-life solutions for building and enhancing oneness in your marriage.

You'll learn:

◆ *Five secrets of successful marriage*
◆ *How to implement oneness in your marriage*
◆ *How to maintain a vital sexual relationship*
◆ *How to handle conflict*
◆ *How to express forgiveness to one another*

Our insightful speaker teams also conduct sessions for:

◆ *Soon-to-be-marrieds*
◆ *Men-only*
◆ *Women-only*

The FamilyLife Marriage Conference

To register or receive a free brochure and schedule, call
FamilyLife at 1-800-333-1433.

FAMILYLIFE

A ministry of Campus Crusade for Christ International

Take a Weekend...to Raise Your Children for a Lifetime

Good parents aren't just born that way; they begin with a strong, biblical foundation and then work at improving their parenting skills. That's where we come in.

In one weekend the FamilyLife Parenting Conference will equip you with the principles and tools you need to be more effective parents for a lifetime. Whether you're just getting started or in the turbulent years of adolescence, we'll show you the biblical blueprints for raising your children. You'll hear from dynamic speakers and do fun parenting skills projects designed to help you apply what you've learned. You'll receive proven, effective principles from parents just like you who have dedicated their lives to helping families.

You'll learn how to:

- *Build a strong relationship with your child*
- *Help your child develop emotional, spiritual and sexual identity*
- *Develop moral character in your child*
- *Give your child a sense of mission*
- *Pass on your values to your child*

The FamilyLife Parenting Conference

To register or receive a free brochure and schedule, call
FamilyLife at 1-800-333-1433.

FAMILYLIFE

A ministry of Campus Crusade for Christ International

FamilyLife Resources

Building Your Mate's Self-Esteem

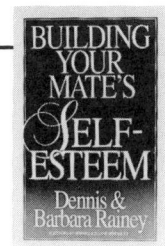

The key to a joy-filled marriage is a strong sense of self-worth in both partners. This practical, best-selling book helps you tap into God's formula for building up your mate. How to overcome problems from the past, how to help your mate conquer self-doubt, how to boost communication, and much more. Creative "Esteem-Builder Projects" will bring immediate results, making your marriage all it can be. The #1 best-seller at FamilyLife Marriage Conferences across America. **Paperback, $8.95**

Pulling Weeds, Planting Seeds

Thirty-eight insightful, thought-provoking chapters, laced with humor, show how you can apply the wisdom of God's Word to your life and home. Includes chapters on making your time with your family count, dealing with tough situations at home and at work, living a life of no regrets, and MUCH MORE. These bite-sized, fun-to-read chapters make this great book hard to put down. **Hardcover, $12.95**

Staying Close

Overcome the isolation that creeps into so many marriages, and watch your marriage blossom! This best-selling book, winner of the 1990 Gold Medallion Award for best book on marriage and family, is packed with practical ideas and HomeBuilders projects to help you experience the oneness God designed for your marriage. How to manage stress. How to handle conflict. How to be a great lover. And much more! Based on 15 years of research and favorite content from the FamilyLife Marriage Conference. **Paperback, $10.95**

The Questions Book

Discover the miracle of truly understanding each other. This book will lead you into deeper intimacy and joy by giving you 31 sets of fun, thought-provoking questions you can explore and answer together. Space is provided for you to write your answers. Share your innermost feelings, thoughts, goals, and dreams. This book could lead to the best times you'll ever spend together. **Hardcover, $9.95**

For more information on these and other FamilyLife Resources contact your local Christian retailer or call FamilyLife at 1-800-333-1433.

HomeBuilders Evaluation

Your First Name _____ Last Name _____

Spouse's First Name _____ Wedding Date _____ Your Age _____

Home Phone _____ Work Phone _____

Address _____

City _____ State _____ ZIP Code _____

Full Church Name _____

Church City _____ State _____ May we quote you?

❑ Yes   ❑ No

How would you rate this HomeBuilders Couples study?

	Poor							Excellent		
Overall experience	1	2	3	4	5	6	7	8	9	10
Study Guide	1	2	3	4	5	6	7	8	9	10
Leader's Guide	1	2	3	4	5	6	7	8	9	10

How many HomeBuilders Couples Series have you now participated in ? [   ]

Describe the effect this HomeBuilders study has had on you, your family and your group:

How would you change or improve this HomeBuilders study?

Was this group formed from your: ❑ Church Community ❑ Neighborhood
❑ FamilyLife Marriage Conference ❑ FamilyLife Parenting Conference
❑ Work place   Other: _____

How many people were in this HomeBuilders group? _____

Where did you meet? ❑ Home (s)   ❑ Church building

How often did your group meet? ❑ Once/week   ❑ Every other week
                               ❑ Every month   ❑ Other: _____

What day of the week would your group normally meet?

❑ Sunday Morning   ❑ Monday   ❑ Wednesday   ❑ Friday
❑ Sunday Evening   ❑ Tuesday   ❑ Thursday   ❑ Saturday

Have HomeBuilders materials been used in your church? ❑ Yes ❑ No

Have you attended a FamilyLife Conference? ❑ Yes ❑ No

Pastor's First Name _____ Last Name _____

FamilyLife has many other resources for you and your family. Please check if
you would like to receive additional information on the following resources:

❑ Other HomeBuilders Couples Series studies   ❑ "FamilyLife Today"
❑ FamilyLife Marriage Conference   radio program
❑ FamilyLife Parenting Conference   ❑ Books, videos and tapes